FRIED SPUDS AT TEN

Other books by the author

FRIED SPUDS
AT
TEN

An Isle of Wight Childhood

PETER G. NEW

Published in 1991 by
The Self Publishing Association Ltd
Lloyds Bank Chambers,
Upton-upon-Severn, Worcs
A MEMBER OF

in conjuntion with
PETER G. NEW
Harpenden, Herts

British Library Cataloguing in Publication Data
New, Peter G.L. (Peter Gold) *1926 –*
    Fried spuds at ten.
    1. Isle of Wight. Social Life, 1901 – – Biographies
    I. Title
    942.28082

ISBN 1 85421 107 2

Designed and Produced by The Self Publishing Association Ltd
Printed and Bound in Great Britain by Billing & Sons Ltd, Worcester.

CONTENTS

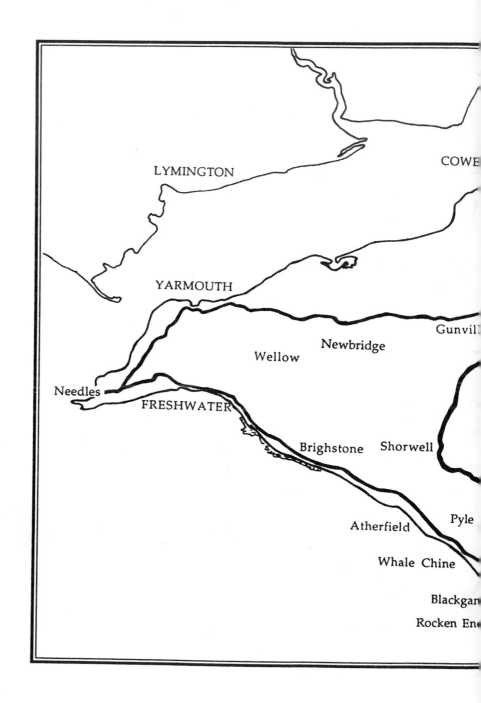

LYMINGTON

COWE

YARMOUTH

Gunvil

Newbridge

Wellow

Needles

FRESHWATER

Brighstone   Shorwell

Pyle

Atherfield

Whale Chine

Blackgan

Rocken En

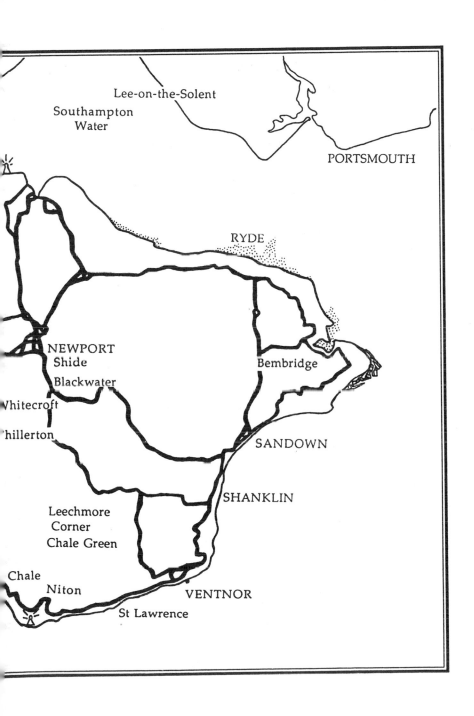

To
BARBARA
who has heard all these stories before

and in memory of TED
who would have reminded me of many more

PREFACE

Lighthearted memories of a peasant youth hardly merit a formal introduction, but perhaps a few words of explanation will be useful. It will be clear from the title I choose that there are few similarities with the high society world of *Carriages at Eleven*.

This is mainly about my childhood years in the Isle of Wight though I take the story on through my brief inglorious service in the RAF and as far as my graduation at Durham. But I do not stick rigidly to this limit. Occasionally I refer to later years, especially when I wish to round out an account of a friend or a member of the family.

It is all true. There is no deliberate invention of any incident, although I cannot guarantee that time has not created its own apocrypha. In most instances the speech reported is clearly remembered, and elsewhere it is to the best of my memory, except that in two places I have, in the interest of an effective description, put words into mouths. (The italics on pages 103 and 163.)

I take a dislike to books which attempt to represent regional accents with strange variant spellings, such as *"tha naws"* for "you know". To those unfamiliar with the accent it is often annoying, and at worst it is incomprehensible. The works of Burns are totally opaque to me for this reason. Yet some suggestion of the local speech gives an authentic flavour to writing in a regional context, and if it were understandable it might have some interest, and perhaps humour, of its own. So here I attempt to get the best of both worlds. I report speech firstly as it would be spoken in Received Pronunciation, then I add, in brackets and in italics, a spelling to suggest how it would sound in Isle of Wight speech. Thus: "I shall have to be going" (*Shlaft'begorn*).

I would be interested to hear from anyone who can offer additions or corrections to my account. Some readers may wish to take this book seriously and even use it as a piece of evidence in local or family history. I have therefore been deliberately profligate with proper names – perhaps a little extra sharpness is thereby imparted to the narrative. In the best traditions of my profession of librarianship, I also add a name index of people and places cited.

But I prefer to think of this book as fun. It was fun to write and I hope it is fun to read.

Harpenden 1990   P.G.N.

CHAPTER ONE

Time and place

Pyle Street runs parallel to the High Street in Newport, Isle of Wight. It is of equal length, and to me as a boy it seemed of equal importance. Newport was my nearest town, and so a model for my judgment: I therefore expected all towns to have a Pyle Street. Strangely I found that Ryde, Ventnor and other Island places did not conform to the rule – they had a High Street but no Pyle Street! Only later did I realise that there was nothing wrong with these towns, but that it was my yardstick which was out of kilter.

I was reminded of this when reading Don Haworth's *Figures in a bygone landscape* (Methuen, 1986). One of Don's earliest memories is of God watching over him. "He had button eyes and red trousers and perched on my cot. By the time the distinction was made between God and Golliwog the image was ineradicable . . ."

Children have insufficient data to compare and evaluate the experiences they encounter. Their vision is sharp, bright, and distorted. Thus first impressions tend to be taken as standards, and a way of life, however bizarre, is accepted as the normal order of things. Youngsters born with silver spoons in their mouths are not aware of their affluence, and poor children are not, except *in extremis*, conscious of their poverty.

We were never *in extremis* but I can see now, if not at the time, that my parents had to work very hard to make ends meet. From when I was six to my teenage years my father was trying to run a free-range poultry farm on four windswept acres at Chale, on the southern tip of the Island. It was doomed from the start. Poultry keeping never became viable until the battery system took over. In any event, the war killed off our efforts because the government decided that it was more economic to import dried eggs than poultry food. So at that stage Pop switched to becoming a mental nurse, passing all his exams at first go at the age of fifty-six.

To supplement income my father occasionally took a second job; gardening, dung spreading on a farm, or helping in the building of the holiday camp at Atherfield a couple of miles away. My mother was a part-time nurse for a while and for most of my childhood let rooms to holiday-makers in an entirely unsuitable house. This venture meant that the family was dispossessed of its normal sleeping quarters: I recall distinctly my father's hoarse whispered enquiry to my mother "Where are we tonight, mate?" Brother Ted and I were frequently consigned to a tent in the garden, sometimes the egg shed. It was all a bit of a lark – any sympathy for a deprived childhood would be quite out of place.

We boys never thought about being poor or rich. But looking back one can pick out some signs. I think it was Miss Pinnock, of the local minor gentry, who complained about the unsightly fencing around our smallholding. Doubtless, bulging wire netting and rough wonky stakes, bark and all, (*zouls* in Isle of Wight dialect) are ugly, but the peasant economy takes no account of aesthetics. We would have thought it the height of irresponsibility to spend a penny more than the minimum just for the look of the thing. We found an old frying pan on the dump (Miss Pinnock's?), and although it had a loose handle my mother used it for many years. Visiting my parents in my twenties, I was disconcerted to be served a kipper on two-thirds of a plate, the juices dripping off onto the table. The comfortably-off may ask why others do not keep up to their own standards; they also ask how people can possibly live on a third or a quarter of their own income. The above examples answer both questions.

Indicators of living standards must be taken in the context of the times. When worried about money, my parents would wag their heads and foretell that (a) we would end up in the workhouse and (b) we would have to use margarine instead of butter. We boys thought the latter a greater calamity than the former, if only because we had little idea what a workhouse was like (though they still existed then). No-one would have dreamed of preferring margarine to butter in those days. Years later, when Pop was working at either Whitecroft or St Mary's Hospital, I remember him saying "I'm earning good money now". It was £6 a week, worth more then than now, but still not princely.

My mother would put the verbal mockers on Christmas ("All a lot of fuss and expense for a few days . . . I'm glad when it's all over . . .") but that did not stop our enjoyment of it. Apart from presents, the highlight was gorging ourselves with nuts. These were placed in a large crock pot, the sort which may have been intended as a bread bin, or used for preserving eggs with isinglass. Ted and I would nag until we gained the official "off". Then the rate of our consumption was limited only by the speed at which we could crack the shells with one pair of wonky nutcrackers between us, and we would fill ourselves until we were painfully distended with wind. (In 1989 I was amazed to find these bent nutcrackers still in use in the family of Ted's widow. They must have assumed their idiosyncratic shape some time around 1930 when confronted with a recalcitrant walnut.)

Yet it is a trace of Puritanism, not hedonism, which survives from my youth. If it is not Christmas I cannot buy myself a bag of mixed nuts from Sainsbury's without a faint twinge of guilt. Similarly I feel sinfully self-indulgent if I treat myself to a coconut. I had been drilled into the belief that the only permitted method of acquisition was by a coconut shy: unfortunately my lack of prowess in throwing meant that I would never get fat that way.

We might have been poor, but we kept up a seemly façade to the rest of the world and we lived under a well-ordered régime at home. We regularly changed our underwear once a fortnight, and to facilitate this the calendar was marked up with 'PV' (for pants and vest) on alternate weeks. Ted, in particular, disliked PV days because he found the newly laundered garments harsh to the skin. The difference between the respectable front to outsiders and the reality among ourselves was understandable if expense was involved, but I noted at the time that we had two sets of manners, one home, one away, so to speak. When, inevitably, we slipped up in front of strangers, my mother would cover her embarrassment with "Kids do let you down, don't they?" But a single standard of behaviour would have avoided these gaffes and would have developed a bit more social confidence.

Our childhood was against the backdrop of particularly dramatic national and international events, but without a basis for comparison we accepted them all in a blasé way. While we played on our poultry field, Europe was appeasing Hitler, then re-arming, then fighting him. We were not entirely unaware: I can still see Chamberlain waving his piece of paper on his return from Munich and declaring "Peace in our time!"

I recall sharply the – to me – astonishing words of Lord Dawson of Penn about George V: "The King's life is drawing peacefully to its close". Astonishing because it seemed to a lad of ten that a doctor, however eminent, could not take the place of God and say when someone would die. I am greatly taken by George V's last words, appropriate in their time, but now so splendidly dated that I may borrow them for my own use if I get the chance. They are "How is the Empire?". (These are the *official* last words; the unofficial "Bugger Bognor!" refers to the location of his last illness.) His son's abdication broadcast was also memorable: ". . . my final and irrevocable decision . . ." His loyal subjects responded informally by singing

Hark the herald angels sing
Mrs Simpson's pinched our king!

And one night in 1936 we saw a great glow in the sky to the north-east, over our goat-shed. It was the Crystal

Palace burning down at Sydenham, a hundred miles away.

In general I was too young to have an *opinion* on world affairs. Thus when I was disciplined at school for shouting political slogans in the corridor I did not know their meaning. My offence was for being noisy rather than being the fascist indicated by the words I used. They were "Tunis! Corsica! Nice!" which were Mussolini's claims on France at the time.

The popular songs of the time are well-known to the present generation, and when they are played nowadays they drip with nostalgia for me. My mother was keen on Gracie Fields, but I could not abide her myself. However, she was such a celebrated figure that when they commissioned a new paddle steamer - the pride of the fleet - they called her the *Gracie Fields*. She would set out from Ryde pier head with the strains of *Sing as we go* or *Wish me luck as you wave me goodbye* in that shrill Rochdale voice (permanently sharp?) coming from a gramophone on the stern. But this was not to last. Poignantly, the *Gracie Fields* was one of the 'little ships' which went down at Dunkirk.

Paddle steamers were used on cross-Solent services and also for 'round the Island' pleasure trips, calling in at the many resorts around the coast (even tiny ones like Totland Bay) all of which had piers in pre-war days. Part of the pleasure of the trip was going below to look at the engines – a magnificent example of massive low technology. Huge cranks rose and fell, driven by gleaming rods coming from the steam cylinders. I was interested to see that at the top of its travel, the crank would flick a droopy piece of flannel which had oil fed to it, and so a dribble would run down to the bearings.

Some of these vessels were built in the nineteenth century, such as the *Lorna Doone* and *Princess Helena*. Ted and I always pronounced the name of the latter *Heléna*, with the accent on the second syllable (like the island St Heléna), perhaps because the rhythm accorded with the throb of those great engines. Most of the paddle steamers went to Dunkirk, and so did the cross-Solent cargo barges, familiar to us when lying on the mud at Newport Quay at low tide. Were the Dunkirk soldiers accommodated in the dark cargo holds, coal-dust and all? In particular I remember the *MFH*: it was some time before I sorted out that the initials stood for Master of Fox Hounds.

War was to us part of the normal order of things. Lying on my back on our field in the hot summer of 1940 I became aware of tiny silver specks weaving and turning high, high in the sky above. This was the Battle of Britain. On weekends the lads of the village would cycle out to see where the latest Dornier or Heinkel had come down, untidily scoring through growing crops with its twisted propellers. In the run-up to D-Day we noticed strange structures floating in the Solent; we had no idea what their purpose was. They were, in fact, the pieces of Mulberry Harbour and the giant reels for the Pluto pipeline. The latter needed a land connection across the Island, and when we asked why this huge underground pipe was being laid we were told it was for milk. . .

One day we got to school in Newport to find that the doctor's house next door had suffered a direct hit. The gruesome effects - the death of Dr Straton and the tattered fabric caught up in the blasted tree in the garden - did not strike home. Instead we welcomed the break with routine, the let-off from lessons. So we spent a happy morning sweeping up broken glass and washing up dust-covered utensils in the school kitchen which was only a playground away from the bomb crater.[1]

Although we may not have had too strong a grip on what was going on in the world, we were inevitably shaped by the climate of opinion prevailing in our time. Britain was the centre of the world. Did not the 0° meridian pass through our capital, and did not the Royal Navy and the Royal Air Force have no need to specify country? Chale School, doubtless like most others, had a shiny American cloth world map which demonstrated the might of the British Empire by the amount of red on it. (Later I discovered that it cheated by using Mercator's projection which exaggerates high latitudes, making Canada utterly vast.)

I assumed that British goods were the best and that the products of other countries were poor copies. We thought the few German Opel cars we saw were tinny and unreliable. I never questioned the supremacy of British civilisation; by the time I learned about Babylon, China, Greece and Rome the prejudice was too far ingrained. For most of my career I taught students from many racial backgrounds and I hope that I never discriminated; but if anyone of my generation did, the

---

[1]   A fully documented account of all these wartime events may be ￮ found in Adrian Searle's *Isle of Wight at War* (Dovecote Press, 1989).

18

blame might be attributed to up-bringing rather than evil intent.

Such chauvinistic sentiments were commonplace at the time, and were likely to be strong in a rural area like the Island. There was an air of Victorianism - in the vintage of many of the buildings, and in the connections with the royal family in the nineteenth century. I just remember the old royal yacht *Victoria and Albert* at Cowes, resplendent with its ormolu bowsprit. And I was intrigued by one of the Island's railway coaches in which the seats were arranged in a large oval: I later found out that this now shabby object was Queen Victoria's travelling saloon, used when she came to Osborne House. We had our own humble connection with royalty. My mother was proud to show me the excellent quality second-hand linoleum she had put down on the kitchen floor. "Queen Victoria walked on this" she said. True or not, she did buy it at a sale at Osborne House.

Of course we children were less concerned with national and international events and attitudes than with our day-to day life on the Isle of Wight. Indeed we became sated with the Island. There is a limited area to explore and we had seen it all several times over on our bicycles. During part of the war there was a restriction on travel in the coastal zone, but the reason we did not venture on to the mainland was the sheer inconvenience of getting a ferry and ensuring that we caught the last one back.

I did go to one football match at Fratton Park to see Portsmouth when they were top dogs of the Football League. This was the era of Scoular, Dickinson, and

Froggat, and the time when Pompey were League Champions for three years in succession. It was near Christmas when a group of us went over, but I forgot the whole episode until forty years later when on a visit to the Island, Fred Prangnell greeted me with the single phrase "Lavatory brushes!" I was puzzled by this until Fred reminded me that on that visit to Portsmouth we had taken refreshment in some café which was decorated with a multitude of small Christmas trees. Apparently I had likened them to lavatory brushes, and by the sort of mischance which occurs at noisy parties, I did so when the whole room had fallen silent.

As I grew up I became more and more sick of the Island. I am sure that youngsters on the Isle of Wight are not alone in feeling that all the action is elsewhere, but with more reason they see that to progress with any career it is essential to leave the Island. So when the time came for me to choose a university (and I was in fact given a wide choice) I chose Durham on the grounds that it was the furthest away from home. Had I known that St Andrews was even more distant I would have gone there (and obtained an MA instead of a BA).

In later years the satiation wore off. With a home on the mainland I went back only two or three times a year to see the family. At last I could begin to see the Island with a fresh, unjaundiced eye. I could even appreciate that Newport, previously thought stale and crumby, was a genuine, untouristy market town with a few fine features. As time went on my feelings became more positive: I looked forward to my visits, not only to see my people but to see *the place*.

When I go down to the Island now I frenetically consume petrol in seeing as much of it as I can. Barbara, my wife, does not fully share my zeal, but she goes along. So we might, for example, travel from Chale to Chillerton, not direct, but via Blackgang, Niton, Ventnor, Shanklin, Godshill and Rookley. A sort of obsessive ritual pilgrimage to pay homage to as many places as can be fitted in. Havn't seen Wellow recently. . .

More sensibly, we take a walk on the downs. From almost any high ground on the Island one can see from side to side - Solent to Channel, Culver Cliff to the Needles. A great sense of geography. Even at the height of the holiday season there are no crowds on the downs, in contrast to the jostling pink multitudes at the seaside at Sandown. Nothing wrong with Sandown, but one beach is very much like another, whereas the downs show the unique form of the Island.

The powerful sense of place I feel is almost impossible to describe, but Wordsworth would have understood it. "Love" is not quite the right word, being mawkish, also too wide and debased in meaning. The feeling is certainly not just an appreciation of the beauty of the Island, but is to do with belonging and a sense of rightness and permanence. Perhaps the best we can do is to say that it is somewhere between yearning, satisfaction and refreshment. But even the most carefully chosen words are a banal description. Better to rely on experience rather than a word picture. Even without being Island born and bred, you may gather what I mean if you wander over Brighstone Down or, from the viewpoint car-park at Blackgang, gaze at the scallops of the coastline all the way down to Freshwater.

I have no doubt that similar feelings are held by others for their own home areas. But one would expect islands to engender a particularly strong sense of place: their individual shape and separation from the mainland strengthen their distinct identities. Their greater or less isolation fosters the survival of their own dialects, accents, surnames, and even ethnic types. At least this is true of the Isle of Wight, even though it is only a mile or so from the Hampshire coast.

But that little strip of water makes all the difference. Grandfather Gold died at Bournemouth, and my parents, brother Ted and I went across the water to his funeral. We missed the last boat back from Lymington, and as it was at the height of the holiday season we could find no beds anywhere, even with the help of the police. In fact we spent the night on someone's sofa and armchairs. Somehow it was all the more memorable because Pop was, entirely against his nature, wearing a bowler hat throughout.

The little strip of water also means that I know scarcely more about Hampshire than I do about Devon or Cheshire. Only now am I beginning to correct this, but in my younger years when I did leave the Island, I got off the boat at Portsmouth Harbour and directly on to the train which would whisk me to Waterloo, so all I saw of Hampshire was from a train window. Not surprisingly, newly-discovered Hampshire and Dorset remind me strongly of the Island, and should I wish to move from my present address to a retirement home, I might choose the Purbeck area of Dorset. It avoids the Isle of Wight's difficulty of access, but has the same downland topography. In fact the geology is the same. Stand on the cliffs near Swanage, look due east and fifteen miles away you will see the Needles, the Island's western tip of the same chalk ridge. Recently I was in Wareham, and the kinship with the Island was uncanny: even the air was Chale-like, mild and moist.

Every time I visit the Island in recent years, its pull on me seems to get stronger, and perhaps after all I might retire there despite the disadvantages. Without a profession to follow, I would find that the Island caters well for my limited interests. I would never exhaust the footpaths, for example; by the sea, over the downs, through forgotten farms. Incidentally, the Island is larger than is commonly supposed by those who have not been there. It is roughly diamond shaped, twenty-three miles from east to west (Bembridge to the Needles), and thirteen miles from north to south (Cowes to Chale). It is not uncommon to find letters addressed to, say, 57 High Street Isle of Wight, presumably in the belief that it is not big enough to have more than one settlement – like Hayling Island, in fact.

All dialects are diminishing fast. In my father's youth, vocabulary and constructions peculiar to the Island were common: his contemporaries had the last chance to get it all down on record before nationwide communications started to blot out the differences. When I was at school one could hear examples such as 'Please Miss, my book's fowsty" (mouldy) – which gives some indication of the inadequacy of the storage conditions at Chale School. And even today, although they will call a spade a spade, you will never hear true Islanders refer to a fork – it is always a "prong". So what do they call the prongs or tines of a fork? Answer: a hayfork (or pitchfork) is a "two-grain prong" while a garden fork is a "four-grain prong". When digging spuds you may impale one on the fork; in Island speech you would wail "Ah! I've pronged one!". Is this the origin of the RAF term "prang" – to crash or damage?

I still have not shaken off all traces of dialect. I believe that my total confusion over "shall" and "will" reflects a different Island usage, and for many years I followed the regular Isle of Wight practice of inventing the words "somewhen" and "anywhen" on the analogy of "somewhere" and "anywhere". To this day I must consciously check to determine which of these words I can use without causing raised eyebrows in educated circles.

An accent is quite a different matter. Accents - merely variant local pronunciations of standard English - are still widespread, putting regional stamps on those who use them. To all but the expert, the Isle of Wight accent is indistinguishable from that in the rest of Wessex, and many could not tell the difference from the speech of Devon or Somerset. It is characterised by sounding medial and final 'r's as in *farmer*. (Not a rolled 'r'; the tip of the tongue curls upwards...) and a flat 'a' (æ in phonetic script) like the Northern pronunciation of *brass* but longer. This flat 'a' disastrously affects an Isle-of-Wighter's attempt at "How now brown cow?" (Æu rather than au in phonetic script.)

Some regional accents are more acceptable than others: Scots is fine, but Birmingham less so, while a Wessex speech suggests an honest but slow country bumpkin.

This is the voice with which I lectured many generations of students. They must have thought me a sort of poor man's John Arlott. Most people will say that they like to see regional accents preserved but extreme cases are not easily understandable (thick Tyneside or Glasgow). I don't think anyone has had that problem with me, but I may have missed the odd job because standard pronunciation was preferred.

On the mainland my eye is immediately drawn to a car with a DL registration, the only letter combination in use for Isle of Wight cars. In the same way my attention is captured by a surname such as Cheek, Downer, Flux, or Sprake; all very common Island names. Westmore is also frequently found: a hairdressing family of this name left the Island and made good in Hollywood as make-up artists. Mew is more usual than New, and my childhood was punctuated with putting people right about my surname. Off the Island some folks half seriously enquire if it is spelt Gnu.

It sounds exaggerated to claim that there is a distinct physical type to be found on the Isle of Wight, and I do not press the point too far. But Barbara has the fresh eye of a non-Islander and she frequently says to me "Look! There's a man just like Pop!". There may be something in my theory because at the time of the invasion of the Angles and the Saxons, the Jutes came too, settling in the east of Kent, around Southampton, and in the Isle of Wight. So Pop was probably a Jute. He was short, had fair skin, dark hair (what there was left of it) and blue eyes. And there are a lot of other Island men like him. Dark hair is common, fair hair a trifle rare. So in my adolescence my natural urges were channelled into a

25

quest for the rarity of blondes. Barbara is a blonde.

I have, however, recently become aware of an alternative, if fanciful, account of how the News came to be on the Isle of Wight. A kinsman, Lee New of Southampton, has spent some years in researching the family tree, and he has unearthed the legend that the first New came ashore "in a trunk". A fanciful story indeed. But it happens that a sea-chest, believed to be Jacobean, has been handed down to the eldest son in our family for as long as can be remembered. (It now belongs to my son Simon, as my elder brother had no son.) Even more recently I have heard that the chest came from the wreck of a ship carrying wines and raisins from Malaga to London and was found (presumably unoccupied) on Atherfield beach on 11th October 1754. Take your choice between the vague and the precise story. Whatever the truth, you may have seen the chest in the Bembridge Maritime Museum, where it was on long-term loan for some years.

CHAPTER TWO

The Steppes

Go up the hill towards Blackgang from Chale Church and on the left you will see twenty-three steps ascending the steep bank. I climbed them countless times as a child. To call the house "The Steps" was obvious, but my mother had to go one better and name it "The Steppes". It was commonly supposed that this was merely olde worlde, but not so. The name was borrowed from Russia and reflected the inhospitable open space we were attempting to turn into a poultry farm. I see that the present inhabitants use the form "The Steps": perhaps the "Steppes" variation was not understood or the look of our field has so changed that it does not apply any more.

My memories are centred here at Chale, but I was born near Newport in a cottage between Shide and Blackwater, living there until I was six. The main exterior characteristic of West Standen Cottage was the gutter line which humped upwards to accommodate the upstairs windows giving the appearance of raised eyebrows and a permanently surprised look. The cottage is still there – modernised, extended and prettified, but still surprised. I am sure that the residents do not squash big black beetles emerging from the heat of the fireplace, as did my father with his slipper.

Recollections of this early period are sparse and a trifle bizarre. My earliest memory is of being given a prize at a baby show: it was a shiny ball and I can recall the crackle of the tissue paper in which it was wrapped as it was handed down to me in my pram. A bit later was the nightly horror of the Picture Which Went Round the Room. This was in reality no more than the shadow of the window frame projected on the bedroom wall when a car passed, but Ted and I would cower, scream, and dive under the bedclothes when the "picture" zipped round the room as the car drew level with the house. I think we had curtains, but they could not have been very substantial.

When we were at Shide we had a wire-haired terrier called Toddy. One day my father gave him a trim: when the clippers approached the vunerable soft underparts Toddy showed some apprehension and was possibly thinking of snapping. Pop tried to calm and reassure him in First World War soldiers' Hindustani: "Cooch nay goolies, Toddy". Another animal memory is of Pop tipping up the water-butt and revealing underneath a writhing pad of bright green frogs.

Echoes of the water-butt still survive. As a small child I would become distressed if my mother went out of my sight, even only to go round the corner of the house to the water-butt. To this day Barbara says "Water-butt!" when I cannot find her (especially when she has merely popped next door for five minutes). Barbara believes that my anxiety on this score stems from the times my mother was in hospital when I had to be boarded out.

I must have been very young when the first such

occasion occurred. I was accommodated with the warm-hearted Constable family at Shide. Mrs Constable was large, jolly and hard-working. She took in washing as well as other people's babies. Mr Constable, kindly and ginger-haired, worked for the County Council as a labourer on the roads. One of the large family was a boy of my own age: I don't remember his real name but he was always called Nugget. Some years after my stay with the Constables they sent us a letter telling us that Nugget was dead. He had been "messing about behind a horse", was kicked and died instantly. Strangely Nugget re-appeared in my life some twenty years later.

It was in 1932 that we moved to our brand new smallholding at Chale. Soon we erected a sign at the foot of our steps to attract custom. It read:

> THE STEPPES
> Bed and Breakfast
> Eggs - Hens' and Ducks'
> Dressed Chicken (Orders taken)

This, together with a blue enamelled advertisement for Mew, Langton's mineral waters, summed up our business.

Chale was more isolated than Shide. For public transport we were dependent on the No 10 bus run by the Southern Vectis Bus Company, because there were no trains in our part of the Island, although a good network of little puffing tank engines covered the rest. (Now the train service is sadly confined to an ex-London underground train running between the ferry at Ryde and the east coast resorts of Sandown and Shanklin.)

29

Otherwise we had to rely on our own resources, which, in my childhood meant walking or cycling. Our bicycles were purchased by mail order from Gamages of Holborn, a sort of down-market Selfridges. Since they cost only £2 17s 6d each (£2.87½), cheap even then, Pop suggested that their brand name 'Conquest' ought to be changed to 'Inquest'. In later years Ted and Pop got motorbikes to get to work and long after that, cars. But it was only bikes at Chale. When Pop had to get one of our goats to Ryde to be mated he had to walk the animal to Whitwell station, some four miles over the downs.

The other transport service was the "carrier" who conveyed goods (not goats) to and from Newport: there were several carriers on the Island, each with a different route. Ours was Arthur Sprake (pronounced Sprak by some, as a point of style) who took our eggs to market. He succeeded his father Perce Sprak who sometimes accompanied him in the passenger's seat. I remember gazing with wonder at the gold sovereign the old gent fished out from his waistcoat pocket to show me. Now we are back to one-pound coins, but they are certainly not gold sovereigns!

Our house at Chale was entirely unsuited to the accommodation of paying guests. Apart from the lack of bedrooms to take both visitors and family, we had only two rooms downstairs, living room and kitchen/scullery. Coming down the stairs one could turn left for the living room or go ahead out of the front door, so if we were to reach our breakfast in the scullery without disturbing the holiday-makers in the living room, we had to exit from the front door and run round the house. We boys were generally instructed to keep out of the way of "the people" as my mother called the guests. (Was the implication that the family were something less than people, one wonders? But it was true that standards for the 'people' – best china, untorn tablecloth - and for the family were different.)

When we first moved to Chale, there was no electricity in the village. On the day it was installed we sat, in the middle of the afternoon, gazing in wonder at the bare illuminated bulb dangling from the ceiling. Gone were the days when a paraffin lamp was brought into the living room at dusk, like some Jewish sabbath ritual. The only lavatory was an outside earth closet – this in a house built in 1932. The sole tap was in the scullery, so that water for washing had to be carried upstairs for the 'people'. Ted and I cruelly mimicked my mother's breathlessness and London accent when she tapped on the bedroom door: "Hot wawta!".

The scullery served the purposes of kitchen, utility room and bathroom. The bath was covered by a hinged wooden lid to create a big bench. When it was up, for bath night, one could see that a message had been chalked on the underside, and by some lithographic principle it could never be erased, so that it stood as a permanent testimony to our idleness. The words were *ARE YOU NAKED?*

Bath night was a weekly mayhem. The whole family might be concentrated into this one multi-purpose room, particularly if there were 'people' in the living room next door. But the main cause of stress was the smoke. Water was heated in a copper; a large open boiler intended primarily for washing clothes. The source of heat was a coal fire under the copper, and the hot water was baled out to the bath by means of a bucket or a basin. The fire infallibly filled the scullery with smoke. Imagine, therefore, two screaming boys, eyes stinging, complaining that the water was either scalding hot or chilly, dependent on the whim of the fire and the direction of the wind. There is a further theme to enrich the symphony. Friday night may have been bath night, but according to the BBC *Friday Night is Music Night*, so superimposed on everything was Anne Ziegler and Webster Booth singing their heads off. . .

Sweetheart! Sweetheart! Sweetheart! Will you love me ever...?

Occasionally there was an alternative to this purgatory. In summer, Mother would sometimes send us down to the shore to have a bathe, to economise on bath water. Odd. I later found that people may have a bath or shower *after* bathing in the sea to remove the salty stickiness, to say nothing of the sand, tar and seaweed. The sea-bathing edict also applied to Pop who dutifully appeared on the beach in his ill-fitting home-knitted bathing costume – brown and yellow horizontal stripes. I have never seen such an unhappy looking bather: he looked like a half-drowned wasp just rescued from some watery trap. He frequently declared that "the News don't take to water" but I saw no basis for any generalisation beyond himself.

Apart from bed and breakfast, my mother undertook the task of preparing roasting chicken for sale, particularly enjoying the anatomical aspects. Her two party tricks were to touch the appropriate organ and make the fowl squawk after death, and to activate the toes of the dismembered feet by drawing on the tendons. The finished birds were delivered to the well-to-do of the district, because in those days chicken was a luxury; by no means the cheap alternative to meat that it is now. Our family enjoyed chicken from time to time, but usually we would have the unsaleable – those with a crooked breastbone caused by flopping down on their perch, those mutilated by a fox, or a boiling fowl at the end of her laying life.

Similarly we were not short of eggs. No matter that they were the broken, the soft-shelled or the pimply-shelled – they tasted just as good. Even the infertile eggs retrieved after a few days in the incubator could be used for cooking. My father had an unreasonable horror of choking on eggshell, so we all inspected the eggs on our plates minutely.

Also, like most folk in the country, we reckoned to grow all our vegetables. Indeed it was a matter of shame to buy in from outside. "Don't tell Pop I've bought a cauliflower", my mother would say. The taste of fresh vegetables can be unsurpassed, but we were subject to the penalties faced by all gardeners: the obligation to eat the produce whatever its condition (cabbage perforated by slugs, lettuce which never hearted up) and a superabundance of a crop to the point of nausea. It seems that country people grow produce for some mysterious atavistic reason not directly connected with feeding themselves. How can they possibly eat all those runner beans they grow?

But we could never get enough broad beans. The

modern tinned or frozen substitutes are acceptable enough but are quite different in taste from those fresh from the garden. The older and the mealier the better, regardless of the tough skins and the black stripe on the end like a dirty fingernail. We would prepare vast quantities for a meal in the expectation that some would be left over. What greater – slightly sinful – delight than to creep into the larder and pinch a few cold broad beans from the colander (and then go back again and take a few more)? At a meal I would eat my broad beans before anything else on my plate: the reason I offered any questioner was that should I suddenly be taken from this world by a coronary I would not have missed the last delights of my favourite vegetable. Ted shared my passion throughout his life, and we even dreamed up some improbable recipes. His wife Audrey called us 'broad bean bores'.

Another plentiful food was potatoes, and again leftovers were budgeted for. A ritual just before bedtime was to sit around the fire enjoying a plate of fried spuds. Indigestible? No-one in the family has ever had the slightest difficulty in sleeping – my problem has always been waking up. (Years later a colleague described my slumbers as 'a short course in death'.) We must have gone to bed very early in those days, because I remember clearly the routine my father followed about fried spud time. He would wind the clock, observe "Ten to ten and all's well", fart, and add "And that proves it!"

Our milk was supplied by our goats: the 'people' were told that they had been drinking goats' milk only after the event. To Ted and me the goats were pets. One day we wended our way to the top of the hill clad in our

34

choirboy cassocks and surplices and carrying the Book of Common Prayer. We were on our way to the goat shed to marry two of the inhabitants.

In true peasant fashion the family reared one orphaned baby goat on the bottle indoors, which effectively gave it the run of the house when it grew up a little. This was Ernest, or Ernie, whose full name was Ernest Henry Flack, the surname deriving from the sound made when his ears were flicked. (I still address any stray goats I meet as Ernest.) When it was feeding time my mother would announce the fact with a frenetic endearment in the form of a rhetorical question: "Did he want botley-botley?" Ernie's response was a series of short appreciative bleats and a rapid whisking of his tiny tail. He was so voracious that we constantly had to replace the teats on the bottle, which were meant for human, not goat babies.

On one of the rare occasions when Pop was ill, the doctor had to be called out. On arrival he left his medical certificate on the bedside table, but soon there was the patter of tiny hooves, Ernie leaped across the bed and the certificate was devoured. Truth *is* stranger than fiction, and less credible. When asking for a duplicate we felt it wise to explain that "the puppy" had eaten the original. Who would believe it if we had to explain away a goat in the bedroom?

Sometimes we harnessed the goats to our home-made handcarts made from pram wheels and old orange boxes, but we found goat power erratic. Shout and belabour as we might, the goats would merely sit in the traces chewing. Then unpredictably they would leap to their feet and charge down the hill with cart and passengers out of control. On one such occasion we went careering towards a panicky group of hens, squawking, attempting flight, feathers flying like confetti. Fellow passenger Albert Barton cried out "Mind that old fowl!" (*Mine that wall vowel!*). Pop said later that he was less angry at our scaring his hens and putting them off their lay than at the description of one of his prime young pullets as an 'old fowl'.

Ted and I found it great fun to bespatter the chicken houses with droppings; being well formed and tacky they would stay put and offer a pustulated look to the observer. Must have been embarrassing when Pop was showing round Mr R.L. Burton, the dapper city-suited representative of Silcock's poultry foods. Also, we would chalk slogans over any available surface – fowl houses, cupboards, the coal hatch, the inside of the lavatory door. Only now and then were we commanded to clean up. The wheelbarrow was emblazoned with the name AULOCH – we just liked the sound of the word (we pronounced it Awlock). Students of history will know that he was the "mad colonel of St Malo", the German officer who made a fanatical defence of that town. So Pop accepted it as the wheelbarrow's name – "Must take Auloch over to the garden to bring back some spuds".

The garden was on the far side of our plot because Pop thought the best soil was there. It was surrounded by tall wire netting to keep the chickens out, supported by "zouls" (rough stakes). It may have kept the fowls out, but the goats were a tougher proposition. They would get their forefeet up on the fence to chew at the bark of the zouls and their weight could easily bring the lot down, and if this happened they would triumphantly waltz in and consume the entire row of broad beans. What greater tragedy? To avoid having to run over to the garden, shouting the while, when an attack was mounted (and doubtless arriving too late) Pop stayed at the house and became a sharp-shooter with my airgun, muttering curses with an unlit fag grimly clenched in his teeth. Oh yes! The goats would eat anything, even a big chunk of my mother's green crêpe dress on the clothes line.

The rest of our four acres was dotted with small chicken houses all anchored down with stout wire over the roof to withstand the gales which frequently swept up the Channel. Of course we used the free range system of poultry keeping – battery farming was not in vogue then – but even so, a multiplicity of small houses was uneconomic. The repetitive egg collecting, feeding, and cleaning out at each site, and the legwork in getting between them made the operation labour intensive. But we felt we had no choice.

Grandfather Gold thought otherwise. Mother's father took up a smallholding very near us for a year or two, and being a smart-arse, thought he could show us how poultry keeping should be done. So he built one enormous house for his fowls; at least he got as far as three-quarter building it, having only the south-western facing front to complete when the inevitable happened. A Great Wind arose during the night, and in the morning we could not conceal our naughty pleasure at seeing all knocked flat.

CHAPTER THREE

Armagh and Porous Pot

I have no connection with Northern Ireland. When Island children speak of their mother they refer to her as 'Our Ma'. The nearest approximation to a spelling of the pronunciation is 'R Mah' and, remembering the flat 'a', you have the same sound as Armagh. To the end of her life I corresponded with my mother as Armagh, showing not only my facetiousness but a certain awkwardness in our relationship. We were not a family to show our emotions, and perhaps I never felt close to my mother (because of her absences in hospital when I was very young?) but her beneficial influence on me was immense. She was the driving force of the family.

She was born Mildred Florence Gold (marvellously dated forenames!) but my father addressed her as 'mate' and referred to her as 'the Missus' to others. The surname made me wonder about Jewish ancestry, but none was known – indeed Grandfather Gold and others would occasionally be guilty of those commonly heard mildly anti-semitic jokes and prejudices. She was the eldest child, and from the age of twelve when her mother died, took much of the responsibility for her father and brothers. The young Mildred came to the Isle of Wight to go into 'service' at North Court, a large house at Shorwell. She was befriended by the cook there, and it was through her that she met her son, my father.

Armagh never lost her London suburban accent, and since it was so patently out of place on the Isle of Wight she was always marked out as a stranger, and perhaps she was never fully accepted. Certainly her accent was a source of merriment to her sons, even more so when she attempted Isle of Wight dialect and got it wrong. Fascinated with words, we would often resurrect a dialect term and use it instead of the Standard English equivalent. One such was 'callards' which means cabbage, broccoli, spring greens. Armagh rendered this as 'cadlers' (*cadlahs*), and we were so taken by this variant that we adopted it for the future, always being careful not to sound the final 'r'.

Her objective in life was to "get on", less for herself than for her sons, and to this aim she brought wit, energy, and persistence. She steered us towards the "scholarship" examination for the secondary school, at a time when just no-one from Chale School considered going beyond elementary education. We boys must have had something to do with passing the exam, but elder brother Ted was the first to transfer from Chale to the secondary school since 1908 (the names were recorded in gilt on a roll of honour), and the very novelty of the translation added to the feelings the village had that the News were a bit uppity. There was extra expense in sending us to school in Newport, and although it must have been extremely difficult, somehow the money was found for a few educational extras – a sixth-form conference in Hertfordshire and a school trip to France.

Perhaps there was a tinge of "getting on" in some of

the contacts she made with (to put it in a very old-fashioned way) those in a higher social station. But some were sheer chance. As a young woman, she was in hospital with Cliff Michelmore's sister, and, towards the end of her life, she was housekeeper at his holiday house in Bembridge. It was at Bembridge, too, that she had two encounters with Prince Edward. The first was a physical contact – as a small boy he cannoned into her shins on his tricycle. The second, years later, was a telephone call in which the caller announced himself by saying "This is Edward". My mother took this to be her son Ted playing the fool, because he never called himself Edward. So she chaffed back in the vein of "Don't be so daft, Ted" until she had the slightly stiff, affronted response, "It's Prince Edward, actually . . ." Embarrassment. Apologies. Wrong number.

She did tend to cultivate the acquaintance of influential people such as doctors and county councillors; sometimes she needed their help, but perhaps they were also valued as friends of some standing, and so were a comfort and support to her. Her last years were spent happily in the company of the Willis Flemings, gentry who were considerable Island landowners on one side of the family and Charringtons the brewers on the other. (Free *cases*, not bottles, of Gilbeys Gin were delivered to them from time to time). Armagh was once their housekeeper at Pyle Manor, the place which gives its name to the street in Newport (p 9). Ever proud of her sons' cleverness, she told the inhabitants my alternative name for their residence – Haemorrhoid Hall. They were Not Amused. Later she was companion to the widowed Mrs Willis Fleming at Rose Cottage, Fishbourne, just by the ferry. I was a little disconcerted at this elderly lady calling me 'Pete' rather than Peter. Only one other person ever did that – my mother.

When Armagh worked at Pyle Manor in the 1960s she and Pop lived at Granfers Cottage, a minute's walk away. It was there that Pop died. Granfers was a thatched cottage fit to grace any chocolate box, but inside it was simple, small, even primitive. When in the bedroom one could see the goings-on in the room below through the cracks between the floorboards – there was no ceiling. And on the corner of the staircase there was a niche in the wall to enable a full coffin to be turned without tilting . . . But in the 1980s Granfers was transformed into a luxury residence, and in 1989 was on the market for "offers over £250,000".

Mother was strictly fair in her dealings with her two boys. When she brought home a bag of sweets they would be evenly divided between us, to the point of cutting a toffee in half if there was an odd number. This is an example of the meticulous even-handedness which was a forming influence in our lives. To this day I am fair to the point of tediousness, and boringly law-abiding. I almost always park legally and I do not often exceed the speed limit – note that I am too honest to claim perfection. One lapse in my childhood was so exceptional that it has seared deeply into my memory. The Chale policeman caught me stealing a swede from a field at Walpan: he merely took my name (which he probably knew already) and told me off, but such was my terror that five years' hard labour would not have been a more effective deterrent against repetition.

Although she held the scales of justice evenly between

41

her sons, Armagh saw the differences between us in too stereotyped a way. Ted was always seen as the practical one while I was the scholar, and although this was not entirely untrue it was too extreme. It put down Ted's intellectual level too much and did not recognise that I can sometimes knock a nail in straight, but showing Armagh some gadget I was proud of having made did not alter her fixed idea. She also persisted in her belief that my Isle of Wight accent was broader than Ted's. This might have been true initially but hardly so when I had the modifying influence of the University of Durham and a career spent in London, while Ted remained on the Island throughout his life.

Her mischievous sons made life difficult for Armagh. She had a cookery book in which she would make marginal notes on the recipes she had tried, e.g "dry, needs eating quickly". She would be embarrassed, when showing the book to others, that comments such as "rotten, needs throwing out of the window" had been added. We were also in the habit of making up our own words to popular songs – for fun or to supply what we could not remember. Unfortunately Armagh was not, on one occasion, aware of what were the real, and what were the invented words, so she found herself singing at a Women's Institute sing-song:-

> Around the Marble Arch
> Around the Marble Arch
> Oh! What a glorious sight to see
> A horse's head where his tail should be . . .

She said that people looked at her a little strangely. But she could make up her own mad rhymes, such as:

Tweedledum and Tweedledee
Went to Newport on the spree
When the spree began to crack
Tweedledum fell on his back.`

My mother was bustling and shrewd, Pop was easy-going and thoughtful: it was inevitable that there was a good deal of verbal clash. There would often be a wail when Armagh came home from shopping, "Oh Harry! You've let the fire out!", but if he had been assiduous in keeping it stoked, the cry would be, "Fire enough to roast an ox!". I remember her repeatedly screaming down the stairs, inaccurate in her fury, "In the table writing drawer!" when Pop could not find some item which should have been in the drawer of the writing table. Another shout was "You vile beast Harry!" which was brought out when Pop had committed some minor sin such as bringing in mud on his boots or farting in bed.

It can be seen that my mother was given to hyperbole. The finest example of exaggerated invective was reserved for the inoffensive little Mr Cooper who was manager of the Co-operative Stores in Newport. The shop made deliveries, and sometimes Mother would find that sultanas had been sent instead of raisins, which would bring forth, "That bloody man in the Co-op needs horsewhipping!". It seemed to me at the time that the suggested punishment was out of scale with the gravity of the offence. Not that Armagh often used a swear-word, being a regular churchgoer, but when she did she would add "and that's swearing!", as though to suggest that those in the circles in which she moved would not know a swear-word if they heard one. She would frequently avoid swearing by the common device of using a substitute word, but instead of bypassing blasphemy by saying "Christopher Columbus!" she would use her own more original and local phrase, "Christchurch near Bournemouth!".

I don't think Armagh had any deep religious belief: her churchgoing was, I am sure, three quarters to fulfil social expectations and one quarter an insurance for the hereafter. She affected to misunderstand parts of the service of Holy Communion. When the priest is kneeling at the altar praying with the words ". . . not fit to gather up the crumbs under Thy table . . ." she supposed that he was doing just that. And she complained that when he offered her the chalice with the words "Drink ye all of this" she got hardly a sip.

Armagh was expert in a trenchant form of expression which managed to put her in the right on any issue. When she went to a strange place, her observation, "Never been here in my life" was said in a way which implied that anyone who *had* been there was somehow defective. Some of the 'people' were described as "north country folk" in a disdainful manner which seemed to expect the most outlandish behaviour. Similarly, if she were offered food which she did not favour, she would inform us, "I don't eat that muck!", making us question whether it was wise to eat this item ourselves.

The sense of the dramatic extended from her exaggerated language to her behaviour. I recall an occasion when Armagh, at lunch, found that she could not be given the lift she wanted on Ted's or Pop's motorbike. The alternative was the bus which left in five

44

minutes. Her meal being too hot, she held her sausage and mash under the running tap, not only to cool it, but to make her point. She took part in real amateur dramatics too (to the embarrassment of her sons) favouring the Buggins comedies of Mabel Constandouros.

Her comments were sharp and her régime was rigid. Someone felt to be lower in the social scale than herself would be described as "common as muck" (a word she loved), while some sanctimonious person (particularly one of a denomination different from her own) would be said to be "steeped in it". Anyone falling a little short of her standards of probity would be branded as "rotten, rotten, rotten to the core". She would acidly observe "Five o'clock's tea time!" whenever there was any danger of delay, and washing would be done on a Monday regardless of the incidence of Christmas, Easter or Whitsun. And loaves were eaten in strict rotation, so that we were always eating yesterday's bread, never the warm crusty loaf baked today. Armagh remained ruled by routine to the end of her life. When Barbara and I came down to visit her we would be bathed in the anticipatory euphoric glow of homecoming. But when we arrived Armagh told us that she would be going out in a few minutes - "Thursday night is my whist night..."

Apart from her passion for whist, one of Armagh's major social interests for many years was the Women's Institute. She would produce material for the weekly market stall, and it was here that she allowed herself her one little indulgence – a meringue made by that unsurpassed local cook Mrs Parker. (With the eggs we had Armagh could make perfectly good meringues, but

45

not of the Parker standard.) My mother was for some time secretary of her local WI and frequently went as delegate to national conferences, writing conscientious reports on them. She enjoyed all this, but her downfall was her sharp tongue. Upset on some issue, she said in a fit of pique that she suspected that the county elections were rigged. The accusation was taken seriously, the County Organiser was brought in, an investigation was made . . . Oh dear!

In retrospect, one wonders more and more how a woman with a history of tuberculosis found the energy not only to work very hard but to engage in a number of pleasure and social activities. It was particularly strange that someone with so many necessary demands on her time – bringing up two boys, the chickens, the bed and breakfast – should add to her burdens by taking a foster child into the family, but this she did, partly perhaps because she had always hankered for a daughter and lacked feminine company. So Betty Cave became one of us for a few years, but I was away from home by then so I did not see much of her. After leaving school she soon found herself working in the United States, and now as Mrs Lau she lives in Hawaii with her doctor husband.

As might be expected, Armagh was always a little breathless, but she enjoyed remarkably good health from when I was about five to the end of her life. She would attribute her success to fresh air, a regimen recommended to her by Doctor Carpenter of the Longford Sanatorium at Havenstreet. He was more than a medical man to her; he was a counsellor and support, and a goat breeder who set us on the same path. For many years Armagh slept outside in a sanatorium-approved shelter

46

open to all the Chale winds. One night she awoke with a start – a slug was crawling up her lip. Throughout her life she never closed the interior doors of her house, and when I tried to shut them I found that they no longer fitted their frames.

Armagh lived until she was eighty, and even the way she died was so characteristically dramatic that it would have pleased her. In 1980 she went on a package tour to see the Oberammergau Passion Play and died a few days later over the border in Austria at Feldkirk – in mountain country which she loved. The reconstruction of events from accounts of fellow tourists, the international phone calls in German, the repatriation of the body in a strange casket – Armagh would have appreciated all this drama.

Pop was a complete contrast to Armagh: where she was bustling he was easy-going, where she was thrusting he was retiring, while she had a shrewd grip on practical matters he was vague, thoughtful, deep. He therefore lost all verbal battles and unjustly was poorly regarded in the family. So he was called Poor Pop, and when our studies in physics had advanced to the appropriate point, Porous Pot. Ted went further and lettered Pop's bath towel LECLANCHÉ which, after all, is a special form of porous pot.

He patently lacked confidence. I have heard him make half-hearted attempts to break into a conversation, and then, when no-one took any notice of him, mutter to himself, ". . . well, I don't suppose it was worth saying anyway . . ." While this might have had a touch of irony in it, he was undoubtedly shy and avoided social contacts

47

where he could. He had to abandon his normal tobacconists, Rugg's of Newport, because the young women assistants were so surpassingly beautiful that he was too timid to go in. So he found another source for his half ounce of dark shag and packet of Rizla Blue papers. And the family noted that whenever he went out he would make a visual and tactile check on the state of his flies – a flick of the hand and a furtive glance downwards.

His reaction to the gentry was to cringe. He told us that when we lived at West Standen he dared not vote anything but Tory in case his employer (Mr J.Y. Jolliffe) found out and he lost his job. Many years later Barbara and I were to pick up Armagh from Pyle Manor in our car. Pop pleaded with us not to take the car up to the door – such a large car would be beyond our station. It was only an old rusty Austin Cambridge, but Pop considered his little A30 the maximum that would be suitable for the peasantry.

But Pop had intellectual potential, a depth of thought, and a feeling for words; qualities which were never fully revealed because of the inhibiting effect of Armagh and his shyness. Evidence of his ability is his passing of the exams of the Royal Psychological Society to become a mental nurse instead of a poultry farmer at the age of 56. But his intelligence was not always appreciated in the circles in which he found himself. When he ventured the opinion that the Chale "air was like wine" it merely confirmed Grandfather Gold's view that he was a simpleton, if not outright insane.

He would sometimes play the simpleton, perhaps to

turn away criticism and avoid embarrassment. *Picturesque* was always knowingly mispronounced *pictureskew,* and on one of the very few occasions on which he chastised me (for sticking a knife upright in the butter and playing gear levers with it) the slap on the wrists was accompanied by "Don't play with the vittels!". Neither 'vittels' nor 'victuals' were words he normally used: the rusticity was to cover his awkwardness.

Pop had some musical ability, although he chose a strange instrument on which to practise, the banjo. He loved the negro minstrel type of music (*Swanee; Waiting for the Robert E Lee; How you gunna keep 'um down on the farm, now that they've seen Paree?*) but that was not the kind of music he played. A modern parallel would be the difference between the music of the Spanish guitar and the guitar of the pop group. He played, from sheet music, tuneful formal pieces written for the banjo. Armagh sometimes nagged him into performing at village concerts. At one which I attended he broke a string whilst in full flow. Whether this was from playing too loudly, nervousness, or just bad luck, he carried off the mishap quite well.

Pop grew up with horses although when they became replaced by the internal combustion engine he converted to being a chauffeur, as he was in the first years of my life when we lived at Shide. His moment of glory in the First World War was when he was the only one in the battalion who could cajole the mule team to ford the Euphrates. To the end of his life he retained some equine expertise in that he often picked winners at the races: unfortunately his bets were so modest ("two bob – 10p – each way") that he never gained much benefit. He occasionally gave himself a treat by going to a meeting at Goodwood on the mainland.

Pop's time as a driver of Mr J.Y. Jolliffe's Bean car at West Standen never made him a confident motorist. Pop and Ted got motorbikes at about the same time. One day I was riding pillion on Ted's bike and following Pop who disconcerted us by shooting one hand up high into the air. When we all stopped we asked the meaning of this strange gesture and were told that in a horse and cart one raises the whip thus to indicate the intention to stop. In later years he sometimes sat with me as I learned to drive. Approaching some hazard on one occasion, Pop slowly observed, in his rustic way, "Ah . . . I should slow down, or stop, or something . . ." By the time he had delivered himself of this opinion we had passed the problem, whatever it was, and I had taken the appropriate action on my own initiative.

Any Island driver can be forgiven for being nervous of venturing on to the mainland. In my father's day there was only one set of traffic lights on the Island – on the hump-backed bridge over Yarmouth Harbour. And there are, of course, no motorways, a fact to be noted by those who call for motorway driving to be included in driving tests. If there is little need to know about motorways, driving on the Isle of Wight has its own hazards and its own technique. The hazards are the narrow lanes and the blind bends, and the technique is to accelerate on the straights and brake on the bends if a reasonable average speed is to be kept up. I first thought Ted was reckless to drive like this; needless to say Pop did not adopt this method and so proceeded about his business at a steady twenty mph.

Atavistic countryman instincts were never far beneath the surface. In retirement Armagh persuaded Pop to go on some Women's Institute coach trip. He startled the coachload of staid ladies by leaping to his feet, thrashing his cap about in the air, and yelling "There he goes!". He had seen a fox, and this was the hue and cry expected in such circumstances. Peasant attitudes to money persisted, too. His mind boggled at sums over thirty shillings (£1.50), so that he had no idea of costs and was always shocked when he was told. Thirty shillings was his weekly wage when we lived at Shide, although the cottage was provided.

On the very morning of Ted's wedding Pop was repairing a hand lawn-mower. The rear wooden roller had broken, and Pop was laboriously making another out of a length of sapling, trying to remove knots, and boring holes for the fulcra with a red-hot poker. Naturally the finished result did not run true, but all this effort was deemed preferable to paying a few pence for a new roller at Arthur Woods, the ironmongers in Newport.

One day Pop was cutting the front hedge, dressed in his usual scruffy attire. A passing visitor leaned out of his car and patronisingly enquired, "I say, my man, can you tell us where we be?" Pop told us that his reply was, "No, but I can tell you where you *are*", though I rather suspect this may have been what he *wished* he had said. Mind you, we residents did feel a bit superior to the visitors. Whatever the weather they could be seen exhibiting much pink flesh in garments which would never be worn in Bexleyheath or Bradford. And we gained much amusement from their mispronunciations. Chale was sometimes rendered as Shale, Godshill as God-shill, and Gurnard as Grunard. Ted and I copied the last for our own use.

The Puritan work ethic inspired the whole family. Pop toiled hard and conscientiously, continuing until after dusk, and allowing himself little time off. He was always finding something that needed doing; often repairs to fences or fowl-houses to postpone the expensive day of replacement. Yet he was certainly happy because he had realised his dream of being his own boss, even though the financial privation was greater than he had expected. Just occasionally he would pause and wonder what he should tackle next. "What shall we do?" was often abstractedly extended to "What shall we do to be saved?" which would always bring forth the answer "Trust in the Lord and keep your bowels open".

Hard worker Pop may have been, but he was a most lethargic filler-in of forms. He would need to be hounded to get started, and the time taken to consider his replies, together with the pauses between his efforts, led to what Armagh referred to, with some asperity, as "the New trademark". This was a pale ochre circle, like a seal, on the document, and was caused by putting down a dripping cup of tea without a saucer. His dilatory habit prevented my going to Australia. There was a wartime scheme of evacuation of children to the Empire under which I was to live with Uncle Harold near Darwin: preparations were well advanced, all my clothing had been marked with A9243, my distinguishing number; but Pop sent the form in late and I did not go.

Pop told us stories of his own childhood at Shorwell,

taking us back into Victoria's reign. He spoke of Duff Harding, who had the fantasy that he could avoid climbing hills by personally tunnelling through them. Go out of Shorwell towards Newport and you will climb Shorwell Shute; down the other side is Cheverton Farm. Duff Harding was heard to go about muttering to himself "Dive in Shorwell Shute, come out Cheverton". This novel fancy stuck in our minds, so much so that Ted and I made an adaptation and set it to the tune of an anthem familiar to us as choirboys:

> Dive in Shorwell Shute!
> Come out Weston Super Mare!
> Dive in Shorwell Shute
> And come out covered in ashes of violets!
> Glory be to the Father . . .

Pop even taught us words to the church bells. The long peal went:

> Why don't you leave my wife alone?
> She is so drunk she can't get home!

While the short one was:

> My father's new dung prong

Some of his expressions were unsuitable for polite society. A useless tool might be "as blunt as a fart", while something irretrievably ruined would be described as "buggered up and clenched". (To clench is to turn over the points of protruding nails so that they cannot be extracted.) And I could not see why the west of England was singled out for stigma when some stench was said to be "like a West Country shit-house". His favourite expression of surprise was "Well I go to Buggery!" – or for greater emphasis, "Well I go to Sodden Buggery!" (Presumably this place Buggery, wherever it is, experiences a heavy rainfall.) Even more bizarre was his comparison, "A is no more like B than my arse is like a wellcrook". I was not too sure what a wellcrook looked like, but I was confident that it bore little resemblance to my father's behind.

One day my brother and I were helping Pop move a fowlhouse. He cautioned us to be careful of the roof because it was "a bit tender". The euphemism sprang from proprietary interest and a peasant reluctance to bear the expense of replacement. Without these considerations he might have used the simile "as rotten as a hen's turd", an apt image in the circumstances. Taken by this phrase, I would croon to myself, to the tune of *You're as pretty as a picture,*

I'm as rotten as a hen's turd...

I doubt if many of his sayings were original creations. Most had been handed down in an oral tradition, others could be attributed to specific people in Pop's past. Duff Harding, mentioned above, was remembered also for his comment on a talk given by an agricultural expert visiting Shorwell – (Standard English) "I knew that already" (*Knowed that avore.*) Some unknown farm worker assured a colleague that he recalled some historical incident with "I remember the time; it was when [the field called] Eleven Acres was [planted with] oats" (*I minds the time; twuz when Lem Acres wuz wuts.*) And a housewife's request to a neighbour going in

54

to Newport to buy her a piece of Russian cord[uroy] with which to mend her husband's breeches was reported as . . . a *bit o' Rooshan card to mend my wall man's britches wi'*. Perhaps it was her husband who feigned being at death's door for the duration of the doctor's visit, but when he had gone cried out to his wife for a piece of the pork she had boiled the day before – "Jane!" *'e zung out to 'is missus, "Cut us off a bit o' that ar (that there) chopperkin y' bwiled yesterdee willee? I be as hungered as a hoss!"*

Another story which Pop told us was about a clash between two farm wagons, one from Bathingbourne Farm near Newchurch, the other from Plaish, not far from Carisbrooke. In Standard English the story begins, "Bathingbourne wagon overturned: the carter from Plaish fought. . ." (*Bangburn wagon wuvverdrayed you: Plash keerter fowt. . .*) One notes the otiose 'you' in the Isle of Wight version, and the astonishing rendering of Bathingbourne by 'Bangburn'. Doubtless the damaged wagons needed to be taken to Newport and properly repaired (*Needs to be took to Nippert and proper compared*).

Pop would also recite extensive tracts of *Robert of Sicily*, a poem learned 60 years before. Also from his childhood he dragged up a biblical phrase, "Saul! Saul! Blindly daring. . . !" and so sometimes referred to his woodworking saws as "blindly darings". He seized on the sentence "War-loan stock eased" from the radio financial reports and somehow appropriated it to refer to making himself comfortable in his underpants. He would snigger happily to himself at this kind of thing, or even break down into helpless laughter. So let us leave Pop, eyes streaming with merriment at one of his own jokes or at some phrase which had caught his fancy.

CHAPTER FOUR

News and Golds

My brother was christened Harry Edward, but since his first name clashed with Pop's he was always called Ted. Not surprisingly, the story of his childhood is the story of mine, and my account of him here is to some extent a record of joint activities, while it will already have been seen that he appears in many of my anecdotes in other chapters. It was only as we grew up that our lives diverged, but even then, rapport was re-established when we met, so that we were soon giggling over the same cranky view of the world and the same play on words.

We were both show-offs. An early memory of Ted – I suppose he was about ten – is of the electric effect he had on a quiet afternoon when Armagh was entertaining her long-standing friend, Elsie Hayles, to tea. Elsie was a spinster, modest, limited, and strictly chapel. She was the maid to Mrs Blake, of Stone Farm at Blackwater, a prim genteel lady who would always greet us on our visits to Stone Farm with "Mmmm . . . And how are the boys?" She mesmerized Ted and me with her black velvet choker – we had never seen such an accoutrement before, and we could not divine its purpose. Just as the biscuits were being handed round on the best china the door burst open, and Ted danced in, naked except for a waistcoat. The effect was not indecent but simply sartorially eccentric because Ted's skinny legs were through the armholes and the line of buttons extended under the crotch and up the front.

A few years later we got into writing spoof advertisements on any sensuous blank sheets of paper we could find. I still have that wartime publication *Aircraft of the Fighting Powers* – the vade mecum of aircraft spotters – which we defaced in this way. The half-title is embellished:

> AIRCRAFT OF THE FIGHTING POWERS
> – But are YOU a fighting power in today's society?
> Or does your breath have a nasty smell?

The advert went on to introduce a potion to cure the condition, and gave an assurance that it would "not stain the uvula nor inner wall of the stomach". (Would this matter, one wonders?). Ted was good at little sketches of those white coated scientists, wagging a scalpel or something at the reader, with a caption such as, "Hear what Dr D. Kay, the eminent laxo-pathologist, says in his new book *Anal freedom* (Chatto and Windus). . ."

We felt that Chatto and Windus was a suitable publisher for that particular title, but in any event we were fascinated by the peculiar name. So much so that we would sing, to the tune of *Weel may the keel row*:

> Chatto's got the Windus
> The Windus, the Windus. . .

But our favourite publisher's name, which invited some

rumbustious action to be set to it, was John and Edward Bumpus. Long before we knew what a publisher was, when we lived at Shide, we would have a tug of war with an old cycle inner tube to the happy cry of "Dorothy S-t-r-e-t-c-h" who was a lady with whom my mother had been in hospital.

I wonder if Ted and I should have become copywriters. Other blank pages of *Aircraft of the Fighting Powers* advertise products ranging from Cornu the New Corned Beef to Manah Valve Grinding Paste for motor mechanics ("It's Post Haste with Manah Paste"). How we hit on the strange word 'Manah' I don't know, but the name spawned a variation, namely Monarch Fish Pastes. The advert for this featured a cod with a crown on its head.

Another relic of childhood still in my possession is the Great Map which Ted drew. The main town on the island depicted on the map was Dobey (Dhobi means washing in Hindustani), situated on an expanse of water known as the Munday Wash, the entrance to which was Dyer Straits, guarded by the Liveran Lights. Dobey was the centre of an extensive railway network. One of our favourite lines went through the following stations: Last Cup, Bladderful, Dyer Straits, Cross Legge, Pynch End, Down Legge, Dobey. (Incidentally Barbara and I called our first house Pynch End, ostensibly referring to 'pinching and scraping to make ends meet'). Another express line went Dashfort, Dunnit, Dobey. Then there were the lines through the big junction of Gore, such as Little Stropping, Pore Edge, Gore, Dobey. And we must not forget the little isolated branch line from Bordham to the Point of Suicide. When we had finished all this we

59

wondered what we should call the island as a whole. It was Pop who supplied the name – The In Continent.

Ted introduced the family to the game Monopoly which was all the rage at the time. We could not afford to buy a set ourselves, so we made our own, and as might be expected, it was an Isle of Wight adaptation, with insignificant villages such as Porchfield instead of Park Lane. We went further and made up cardboard screens to hide our money, and these were in the form of estate agents or banks. A notice on the side of the bank read:

> The Bank regards as an Unfriendly Act
> any attempt by customers to Peer into
> the Vaults.

I was to become a librarian and a teacher of librarianship, while Ted pursued the very different occupation of electrician. Yet we had the same starting point, and one wonders how far our different lives depended on innate abilities, choice, or circumstances. Long before I had any thoughts of librarianship as a career we created our own library at home, and Ted was at least as active as I was. Not that we were great readers, but miscellaneous books came our way from the house sales my mother attended so regularly, and the motivation was to *organise something* rather than to reflect any studiousness. I was to detect the same motive in myself years later when I took up librarianship for real. In any event I still have some books from our childhood collection, numbered in Ted's neat hand, and lettered "Freelireed Library" with a John Bull toy rubber printing set.

A few years afterwards I was grateful for Armagh's

habit of going to house sales, for at a time when many books wanted for university study were out of print, I was able to pick up some Oxford standard authors very cheaply. There were not enough books in these house sales to attract specialist book buyers, and so they were tied up in lots of perhaps twenty miscellaneous volumes. This meant that to get my Oxford Shelley I had to accept 19 unwanted items. By this method the Freelireed Library became strong on Atlantis and the occult. When we were at Whitecroft Farmhouse we had plenty of room in the attics to house the library. We even had an almost complete set of the early nineteenth century Rees' Cyclopaedia (about twenty large volumes), but had to dump it some years later when we moved to a smaller house. Not long after that the City Librarian of Westminster mused in a professional periodical that he would love to get his hands on a copy of Rees . . .

In later life Ted followed the Freelireed tradition by making a tidy catalogue of his gramophone records. He had quite a good collection of the old seventy-eight rpm discs, all of classical music. To play them he had a somewhat crude-looking, but effective player – crude because Ted had made his own wooden case to contain the working parts. The finished job – painted sticky black – lacked that professional look, and Ted dubbed it 'the musical fowlhouse'. Two days before I write this paragraph I was helping Ted's widow clear out a mass of discarded items at the back of her garage prior to moving house, and, yes, there it was, dusty and forgotten for nearly twenty years, the musical fowl-house.

I think Ted must have developed his musical taste when he was in the Air Force. He told the story of when he was playing a Mozart record to himself in his barrack hut. When it had finished he rushed outside, in his enthusiasm (and desire to show off) shouting "Good old Wolfgang!" He said that a serious youth, hearing the joyful cry, approached him, and from this meeting grew a musical appreciation society. He could shout his criticism too. Many years later he lived at Chillerton, just under the television transmission mast on top of Chillerton Down. I have seen him, when he was fed up with the evening's viewing, go outside the back door, shake his fist at the red lights visible on the mast, and declaim into the night, "A load of old rubbish you're putting out tonight!"

Both of us could combine a genuine love of music with our facetious natures. To the theme of one of the movements of *Eine kleine nachtmusik* we set words deriving from the 'mad colonel of St Malo' who had given the wheelbarrow its name (p36):

> He's just the maddest type of colonel
> He hies from Shepherd's Bush . . .

Shepherd's Bush was selected as being a suitably strange name, but it had no Island connection, so it was soon replaced by Whiteley Bank. As any Islander will tell you, Whiteley Bank is a totally dull crossroads just outside Shanklin. Nothing happens there. But that piece of Mozart was from then on always referred to by Ted and me as the 'Whiteley Bank movement'.

At the time of the Freelireed Library Ted's handwriting had suddenly changed from untidy to neat – something to do with puberty, I suppose. Perhaps his greatest calligraphic achievement was his mock historic document. While she may have had every reason, Armagh could be, like her father, a moaner. One of her typical plaints went something like this: "Whereas I try my hardest to keep the place up together a bit, and all I get is cheek and swearing . . ." So all this was lettered beautifully with the initial "Whereas" engrossed at a huge size and splendidly curly, just like a royal charter. Unfeeling? Perhaps, but we found that this sort of guying turned away wrath, Armagh joining in the laughter.

As Ted grew up he showed the same interest in words and delight in association of ideas which was characteristic of Pop. He would deliberately use dialect words, such as "bivver" (shake, vibrate) or "shotter" (scatter, especially spill accidentally). If Ted found himself in an embarrassing situation (for example if the 'people' had seen him fliting out of his bedroom partly clothed) he would describe himself not as "caught", but "ketched". And if he had found anything he had been searching for, Ted, like any Islander, would call out "Got 'n!" (Got him!). But Ted would go further. As Gotten Farm is next door to Bramstone, the cry would be "Bramstone!" or even "Bramstone Pickle!".

By the same token the fowls (*vowels* in Isle of Wight accent) were referred to as "the consonants", and ball bearings were "godfreys", because Sir Godfrey Baring had been chairman of the local magistrates for many years. I now follow the tradition by calling my mallet Shepton. When going out to cut the lawn Ted would announce that he was about to "cripple the fescues". Talking of lawn-mowing, he called one of his motor machines Satan – because it was a *devil* to start. I'm not sure if that was the mower he fitted with a monster 250cc motorcycle engine, which at least was heavy enough to give the lawn an exceptionally good roll, rendering all molehills glossy flat.

Although Ted was an electrician for almost all his adult life, he started work in Morey's timber yard in Newport. His immediate boss was named, I believe, G.N. Rogers, and he had the occupational disability of all saw-mill workers – four fingers on one hand and three on the other. He was also a lay preacher, an interest which gave a bible-thumping flavour to his ordinary speech. Even "I must look out some oak knees for Clare Lallow" had an apocalyptic tinge, though the meaning was not as opaque as it may seem. Clare Lallow was a Cowes boatyard and oak knees are naturally bent pieces of timber useful in yacht construction. Another saying, which Ted loved to imitate, was "I took a piece of elm home to burn, and I was amazed!" (as though at the Glory of the Lord). The point of the remark was that elm does not normally make good firewood.

After Morey's, Ted went on to work briefly for the Southern Electricity Board and then, for the rest of his life, for Saunders Roe, the flying boat manufacturers at East Cowes. The main post-war project was the giant Princess flying boat, but the problem of insufficient power could not be overcome, and the prototypes could be seen for some years, cocooned and bobbing on the water at the mouth of the Medina. After that, the day of the flying boat was done, and the company became the British Hovercraft Corporation, now under the control of Westland.

Ted, although my elder brother by three years, did not marry until thirteen years later, but his wedding was worth waiting for. At the time my parents were living on the ground floor of the old rectory at Chale, and had the major part of the garden, so that a marquee could be erected for the purposes of the wedding reception. This allowed the family to do much themselves – decoration, the bar, some of the catering – and gave an agreeable, informal, country show atmosphere. All the village was there, although some guests had to nip home in their finery to do the milking before returning to the serious business of boozing. Predictably three village topers were, at a late stage, found asleep together in a heap.

Ted built his house with his own hands – almost completely. He had help from his brother-in-law who was a builder, and one or two specialist craftsmen. After a few years one room was converted to be the village Post Office and shop, bringing in a little extra income, but only at the price of a disproportionate amount of work and a total tie to the premises. Perhaps the building of his handsome and substantial house symbolised Ted's outlook. He preferred to be a respected figure in a limited environment rather than lose identity and standing in a wider field. So he never left the Island but was a leader in his village. He was certainly the major pillar of Chillerton Working Men's Club, and when he died they named a new snooker table in his memory. He would have liked that.

Like all villagers Ted tended his garden: it was less a hobby than the expected thing to do. He benefitted from the deep dark topsoil which had washed down into the valley over the centuries. When Barbara and I visited

65

him at Chillerton a special picking of broad beans was made in our honour and for our return the car boot would be loaded with produce. While the emphasis was on vegetables, flowers graced the front of the house, but unidentified roses were given invented names such as "Dr Crippen" and "Windbreaker". (To this day I follow the same tradition: I do not know the name of one of my roses so I call it "Dunno", and another shrub has the label "Buddleia 'Salterton'"). When Ted was terminally ill he was talking to me about his plans for the garden in the following year. But I knew, and I am sure that he knew, that there would be no 'next year' for him.

Ours was not an extended family. Outside the quartet of Armagh, Pop, Ted and myself we did not have a large number of relations, and those we had were seen only from time to time. Probably the most frequently visited were Grandfather and Grandmother New, who lived at Shorwell, within easy cycling reach for Ted and me on a Sunday afternoon. They lived in a new house costing £700 which they had bought from savings accrued from taking in washing, and accumulated in a teapot on the mantelpiece. (In 1989 the house was on the market for £175,000.) Grandfather was like a biblical patriarch with his venerable manner and white beard, and appeared to do nothing except sit by the fire and minister to his pipe. He had been a carter at Newbarn Farm, a respected job in agricultural circles. As we were about to go he would always give the same puzzling advice, that we should, on our bicycles, keep to the "loo" (lee, or sheltered) side of the hedge. We gave up the attempt to tell him of the rule of the road. . .

George New was born in 1855, married Harriet

Westmore (splendid Island name!) in 1885, and died in 1940. *His* father, William, was born in 1823, and his grandfather, John, in 1788. In some ways it is easy to trace one's ancestors on the Isle of Wight. Country families did not move much before the twentieth century, and there are a limited number of parish registers to consult on the Island. In any event I knew that the News had been Shorwell based for some generations, so I was able to get back to 1815 (John's marriage to Mary Spanner) in no more than an hour or two at the County Record Office at Newport. But I was looking only for the single line of father, grandfather, great-grandfather.

My relation Lee New of Southampton has, by contrast, spent years in exploring the New family tree, investigating many branches. He told me that my great-grandfather's brother-in-law (who had the distinctive name of Moses Munt) was a brave lifeboat coxswain who died at the wreck of the *Sirenia* in 1888. I am rather proud of that, but otherwise I know of nothing noteworthy in the history of the News.

My grandparents' children were William, who was killed in the First World War, my father Harry, Auntie Nellie, and Uncle Fred. Uncle Fred ran a market garden business at St Lawrence near Ventnor, and was, it seems, more successful than we were with poultry. It was he who suddenly upped and ran off to Cornwall with his Landgirl, since when nothing was heard of him. It was said that the most painful part of the whole episode was that he took the best lorry with him.

When my mother went into hospital for the second time, I was sent to stay with Aunt Nellie. She was married to Jim Salter, a farmer, and lived at Vayres Farm near Gatcombe. She was kindly, practical, intelligent, and generous - it was always *two* fried eggs, not just one. Across the valley was another farm, inhabited by one Coster. Coster and Uncle Jim would each stand outside his back door and take part in a bellowed conversation, avoiding the tedious trek down and up to the other's house, but imposing fearsome strains on the vocal chords. Aunt Nellie lived until well over ninety, outliving her brother, my father, by nearly twenty years. At his funeral her practicality came to the fore. We were slowly proceeding through Newport in the cortège on the way from the crematorium when Aunt Nellie became a little agitated, wondering whether she should ask the driver to stop so that she could do a little shopping. I sharply recall that it was a file she wanted from Arthur Woods, the ironmongers. Pop would have approved of her total disregard for the suitability of things.

On the other side of the family we have already met Grandfather Gold who had such misfortune with his ill-conceived giant fowlhouse when he took a smallholding near ours for a year or two. This was enough to make anyone miserable, but Grandfather Gold was a moaner all of the time. He prefaced every remark with a moan, a long drawn out 'oh' (not 'ooh') as in "Ohohohoh"! The bills are appalling!" – which I clearly remember him saying. Even pleasant events were accompanied by a moan. My mother had given her father some pork bones (What does one do with pork bones?). Mother told Ted and me to go up the road to ask Grandfather how he had enjoyed them. So dutifully we enquired: "And how were the pork bones, Grandad?"; to which we had the reply: "Ohohoh! They're lovely, tell Mother". This response is now firmly embedded in the family's vocabulary as a catchphrase. He was not only miserable in his speech but had a jaundiced view of the world and its people, even the family. I treasure his remark made when he heard I was going to university – something about a silk purse and a sow's ear.

Grandfather's wife had died when my mother was only twelve, and he had married again disastrously. At least, almost everyone considered the marriage disastrous and he must have thought so himself for most of the time because the majority of his second marriage was spent apart from his wife. My mother loathed Stepmother as she called her – the word denoted the relationship, but the connotation of the tone in which it was uttered was pure hatred. We rarely saw her, but she did appear, uninvited, at my own wedding – the Spectre at the Feast. We saw her son, Kenneth, once at Chale. He told Ted and me to "Go and fry your face!", a remark we found not only rude but quite un-Chale-like, redolent of his pretensions to an unrealistically high standard of life. He now lives in New Zealand.

Surprisingly, Grandfather was not alone when he was at Chale. He had with him an assistant or companion who must have had the most extraordinary reserves of tolerance to put up with him. This was Fred Bailey, who, we found, also had a remarkable gift of story-telling; so much so that Ted and I called him Bedtime Story Uncle Fred (to distinguish from the real Uncle Fred who ran off with the Landgirl). His story was a long serial, original and totally absorbing – I could not tell you the plot, but I know that it concerned the Argentine Prospecting Company. Fred was a strong Christian: we were fearful when he picked up to read one of our books in which we had written a few rude words, but when he found them he said nothing, slowly taking out his fountain pen, unscrewing it, and crossing out the offending words, all in silence. Underplaying can be so effective. . .

Apart from her half-brother Kenneth, my mother had two full brothers, Jack and Harold. Harold was pushed out of the family nest at the age of fifteen and sent on an emigration scheme to Australia where he remained for the rest of his life. In succession farmworker, goldminer (what an appropriate surname!) and government roadbuilder in the outback, he was tough, resourceful, and completely Australian. We were very glad that we could go out to see him in 1981: my mother and Uncle Jack had died the year before, so he was the sole survivor of the brood.

Uncle Jack demonstrated to me a higher lifestyle, even though he did not have a particularly well-paid job. He was a mental nurse, and his wife (Aunt Hilda) had been in the same occupation, and it was their job which was to be the example followed by both my parents. The reason for their relative affluence was that they had no children, delaying before the war, and then deeming it too late to start a family when Uncle Jack returned from abroad afterwards. So their little suburban semi near St Albans was always neat and they seemed to want for nothing. Only much later could I see how relative the affluence was.

Uncle Jack was quick and intelligent and found that his working life did not extend him fully, except, perhaps, when he was a quartermaster-sergeant in the army. So he had an excess of energy which he put into football refereeing, a local friendly society, ingenious devices for the house or bright ideas which he sent to manufacturers. An example of the last was the suggestion that cooked beetroot should be canned in jelly rather than liquid vinegar to save red spills on the tablecloth. Crosse and Blackwell told him that they could not make use of the idea for some reason, but to show their appreciation they sent him a case of their products. Uncle was shrewd enough to get several free gifts in this way or by sending fulsome praise of some product to the maker.

When he retired from mental nursing Uncle Jack had a house built on a fairly big plot of land – again near St Albans – and kept chickens (these two occupations run through our family!). Chickens are a tie, and it was very difficult to get away for a holiday, so as Barbara and I lived not far away at this time, we occasionally moved in to "chicken sit", or look after the 'gregories' as we put it (Gregory Peck). We were in fact UJ and AH's closest relations, certainly geographically, and, since there were no children we were to some extent substitutes.

The lack of children became poignant at the time of Uncle Jack's last illness and death, only a few months after he had been widowed. He was then living fifty miles away at Northampton. We were the sole family support in his illness and I was his executor after his death. The thin attendance at his funeral was chilling.

CHAPTER FIVE

Children's games

Like many children, Ted and I were given to lavatorial humour. We were not discouraged by our parents, even if they did not positively urge us on. Perhaps this was a sort of bargain to reinforce the family embargo on talk of things sexual and emotional, not that any suasion was necessary. All of us kept our emotions to ourselves (people who kiss as a greeting still fill me with horror) and while Ted and I might have indulged in sex talk with others we certainly did not with one another. Much too embarrassing. So we plunged into the excretory with extra zest by way of compensation.

Many are the songs or hymns we modified because we did not know the words, or because we thought our version was funnier or ruder. A mild example from the legions we defiled is our adaptation of *As time goes by* (memories of Casablanca, Bogart, Bergman, and "Play it again Sam!"):

> You must remember this
> I want to go to Liss. . .

Liss is a little Hampshire town on the railway line from Portsmouth Harbour to Waterloo with a name which can conveniently be misheard. But not all our adaptations were rude: another Hampshire town was commemorated in:

I Havant said thanks for that lovely weekend...

And sometimes our lyrics gave a hint of the times in which we lived. The Latin version of the carol *O Come all ye faithful!* was rendered by us not as *Venite adoramus* but by *Benito ignoramus*. The only reason for using Mussolini's forename was that it sounded right.

Another reason for composing our own words may have been a reluctance to face up to the sentimentality of the original, and a desire to mask our embarrassment in banality.

Keep the home fires burning
While our hearts are yearning
Turn the lampshades inside out
Till the boys come home.

I can still hear Richard Tauber, then in his heyday, singing the gorgeously romantic *Vienna, city of my dreams*. But we (I think the words must have been Ted's) reduced it to:

Hail! Hail! The end of time!
Peter has spoilt the pantomime
O what a sell he's in the show
Because he has spoilt it they gave him no dough

Looking back after all these years I cannot suppress a trace of amusement at the unspecific nature of the damage I am alleged to have done to the pantomime, while others may very understandably cry "Desecration!" and declare that precious music is ruined by such bathos. But to me the words of a song are totally unimportant. I can sing these daft words in my bath and still glory in the beauty of the music. After all, my voice is the only musical instrument I can play, and words, however crazy, give me more scope than whistling or la-la-ing.

It was not too easy to follow the real words of a song on the radios of the day. They were of distinctive design: the modernistic dome-shaped Ekco (a very early use of plastics) is now a collector's piece. Our set was a Pye, the plywood case featuring the rays of the setting (or rising) sun. Unfortunately the whole thing vibrated at a certain pitch, blotting out vital words. Thus

> Chinatown, my Chinatown
> When the lights are *brrrrr*

And I gathered that the missing word was 'frown' in

> We hope the programme hasn't caused a *brrrr*

because it was the only feasible rhyme to

> 'Cos Monday Night at Eight is closing down

An alternative to radio entertainment was the cinema. My mother directed us towards the Will Hay films. She considered these "laughable", and, of course, they were totally non-sexual. Our reading was, so I recall, confined to the "William" books of Richmal Crompton. I am not certain why we were so unadventurous, but until I was in the sixth form no-one offered any reading guidance or stimulus. My mother wanted her boys to "get on", but the atmosphere in the house was not conducive to study, not only because the one heated living room had too many distractions, but because there was no real understanding of reading as a normal, regular activity. So our imaginative energy was diverted into devising our own stories and games, some lavatorial, none sexual.

One book we did read was the *Mother Goose Book of Nursery Rhymes*. This was illustrated with strange nineteenth-century drawings, for example of gents with crumpled top hats, very long chins and shoes with absurdly curly toes. The text consisted of extremely brief verses of monumental banality, thus:

> Three straws on a staff
> Will make a baby cry or laugh.

or

> Queen Anne, Queen Anne, she sits in the sun
> As fair as a lily, as brown as a bun.

(Which did not stay unmodified for five minutes.)

I believe that the earliest of our own inventions was the Mad Club. This was a collection of drawings of mis-shapen creatures with limbs in the wrong place – some had legs coming out of their head, some arms from their back, and, of course, one had his private parts lolling out of his earhole. One was called the Mace because he was attached to a wooden handle like a truncheon, and his fate was to be flailed about to wallop the others.

A more long-standing part of our mythology was the saga of Sid Strongarm. The story was that he was taking part in an air race, and, feeling hot, took off all his clothes, which – alas! – slipped out of the open cockpit.

When he landed he covered himself with a map to face the reception party and made a little embarrassed speech. Two of the things he said were "I'm not a very good speaker" and "That just about covers everything". One of his listeners – the peppery and wheelchaired Colonel C.Z. Baxter – immediately responded to the latter with "Not quite man!", prodding at the lower edge of the map with his stick. Regarding the former, many years after Sid was invented Ted was attempting to repair a loudspeaker but was not having much success: as he put it, the trouble was that it was a Strongarm (not a very good speaker).

Still in the realm of the fantastic was the game we devised using Armagh's hand sewing machine called 'Motoring through Gunville'. Gunville is a small suburb of Carisbrooke in the centre of the Island - as far from any water as it is possible to be – and is the object of a standing joke about 'Gunville Harbour'. So we would draw an elaborate street plan of our large city of Gunville, and then would attempt to follow a route using the sewing machine with no thread in it, so that it would merely perforate the paper to show our track. It was a two-person job: one would steer the paper under the foot of the machine, the other would turn the handle and so control the speed, varying the pace to add to the difficulties of the steersman. The map, too, would be drawn with a testing of skill in mind. A special hazard was a hairpin bend on which was situated the Bulina China Shop. A crash at this nodal point would render us helpless, near incontinent, with laughter.

Certain mythical Gunville streets and the businesses on them became well known to us. For example, there was the Boulevard, on which could be found Frodun and

76

Chancet the solicitors. The Hard ran along by the harbour: we pinched this name from Portsmouth (At the Guildhall there was a bus stop labelled 'Queue here for the Hard' which rudely intrigued us.) By far the most important company was Mauné-Mumford Aviation. This Anglo-French concern was paralled by another run by a brother and a cousin which produced pig and poultry foods. (Thus our obsession with aircraft and our background in poultry keeping were brought together.) The link between the two companies was the slogan for the chicken feed "Flown in aircraft", because the special Aerated Mash was towed around in gliders to make it "light and digestible for the fowls" as Ted's publicity blurb put it.

Mauné-Mumford gave rise to two songs, the first based on *Camptown Races*:

> Samuel Mumford sing this song
> Doo-dah, doo-dah
> The factory's five and a quarter miles long
> Doo-dah, doo-dah day.
> The workers work all night!
> The workers work all day! . . .

The other was an adaptation of *The last time I saw Paris*:

> The last time I saw Mumfords
> The firm was going strong
> But now it has been knock-ed flat
> All by a flying bomb.

Apparently the bomb hit the very end of the long building and blasted over the end wall. In falling it hit the next transverse bulkhead, that in turn catching the next, and so on for the whole five and a quarter miles, so that the entire building went down like a pack of cards. Barbara reminds me that the dramatic collapse of the Mumford building was one of the first pieces of mythology I imparted to her after we met.

Quite often our activities were less wildly imaginative and more like the normal pranks of childhood, as when we parachuted Marrowfat the cat out of the bedroom window. We were perfectly scientific, and took all the proper precautions. First we found a stone of the same weight, establishing this by placing it on the weights side of the scales while the scrabbling cat was more or less contained in the scoop. Then we attached the stone to a string harness and the parachute, which was a Scout's kerchief, about a metre square. We lobbed the lot out of the window, and all went well, the chute sinking slowly, and with some dignity, to earth. So we sought out Marrowfat, attached him to his harness despite his protests, and launched him forth. Unfortunately there was a malfunction and Marrowfat descended at the full speed of gravity, landing in a clump of Michaelmas daisies and sloping off, unhurt but growling, trailing harness and kerchief behind him.

Pop was responsible for naming the cat. When a tiny kitten he had held it on the palm of his hand, and, influenced by its shape, just said "Marrowfat", and the name stuck. A marrowfat being a type of pea, Ted and I soon extended the name to Marrowfat Pea or Marrowfat P. Now he had a forename and an initial, presumably of a second forename. All he needed was a surname, so we soon supplied one and the name then became Marrowfat

P. Fignfelloe. To complete the picture we looked for a middle name beginning with the initial P, and eventually came up with Phosgene. It was, perhaps, strange to call a cat after a poison gas, but in wartime we were told that a characteristic of phosgene is that it smells of musty hay, and Marrowfat, being a country cat, often whiffed that way. So that is how Marrowfat Phosgene Fignfelloe got his name – which was often shortened, for everyday purposes, to Fos. Another cat was Ewbank Osgood, the first name from the sound he made, the second a distorted endearment.

Twister, our dog, was dubbed by us Otto Van Kragger, or OVK, I don't know why. He was a cross between a collie and an Airedale and we thought him very handsome with a bushy sickle of a tail and a laughing face. Armagh entered him in an informal contest in some carnival or village show. Various prizes were on offer, and we hoped for that for The Prettiest Dog. Alas! In parading around the ring Twister developed an itch in the backside which he relieved by scraping his bottom along the ground while continuing to walk with his front feet (a method of locomotion we called 'bum-paddling'). That settled our chances for the prize for The Prettiest Dog, but we did win a big bag of dog biscuits for The Funniest Dog. They must have thought it all a party trick.

I don't think Douglas the duck counts fully as a pet because he was with us for little more than a week. For some reason he was motherless and the only success of his clutch of eggs, so we reared him on the hearth, in true peasant style. He was tiny, fluffy, and vociferous. Pop told us that ducklings can swim at ten days old, so promptly on the ninth day we floated Douglas on the rainwater butt. He paddled around quite successfully, albeit quacking apprehensively. Since we had been a little premature, we took good care to dry him thoroughly, leaving him to finish off in the fold of the roller towel. Then we forgot about him. Out of kindness, perhaps, we were never told the details of Douglas's demise, but I guess that someone yanked down the roller towel to get a clean section, and Douglas was thrown out to be trodden underfoot.

We had extensive areas for play on our doorstep at Chale. Dangerous though it may have been we spent a lot of time on the cliffs in mock warfare or building "forts" from the driftwood which was found in abundance on the shore. Or we would sit on the very edge of the cliff and hack away with our heels at those round cushiony tussocks of sea-pinks. The object was to send them hurtling over the cliff, preferably to land on a courting couple on the shore below.

Our particularly favoured terrain was the undercliff – the ledge halfway down the cliff formed by a landslip, and Chale was prone to this phenomenon. We would go down a road called the Terrace which runs out directly towards the cliff edge: at its end a steep path to the right ran down the face to some fishermen's cottages on the undercliff. One of these was occupied as a retreat and love-nest by Uffa Fox, the renowned and eccentric Cowes yachtsman who, *inter alia*, taught the Duke of Edinburgh the finer points of sailing.

To the left a little lane went some 50 yards to the village dump where folks tipped their unwanted items over the cliff edge, and where we took delight in retrieving them. Recently I have discovered that previously this lane went on for miles along the edge of the cliff then under Blackgang Chine on the undercliff before joining the old main road to Niton (before the 1928 landslide). Also from the end of the Terrace a drive ran to a substantial house called Lowcliff, but there was no trace of house or drive when I was a boy.

Nowadays not only the dump and fishermen's cottages but three of the Terrace houses have fallen over the receding cliff, and are marked only by clumps of brick, window frames, and crazily lodged garden plants seen dizzily below. A year or so ago I noted that the only trace of No 3 (Seacroft) was its garden gate being used as a makeshift barrier to stop onlookers falling over the cliff, but on a more recent visit I saw that a little more has gone over the edge: the gate can be seen lodged on a ledge below. No 4 (Heathercliff) is the next to go; it may disappear in the next wild storm, or it may survive for half a century. These house names are familiar because we regularly delivered dressed chicken to these addresses.

In our youth we could climb down through the dump to our undercliff adventure playground and if we wished we could pick our way across to the foot of Blackgang Chine, that tourist honeypot, and gain illegal entry. In those days Blackgang really had a chine – a cleft in the cliffs which was heavily wooded, laced with footpaths, and peppered with rustic look-outs. Near the entrance on the road at the top there was a bazaar and 'amusements' (we found the funny mirrors hilarious).

But the Blackgang Chine proprietors (the Dabell

family) could not defeat the forces of nature. Year by year their assets slipped into the sea and during each winter frantic efforts were made to repair and join up broken paths in a chine which was getting smaller and smaller. We noticed that the centre of gravity of the whole operation was shifting to the bazaar and entrance area, and even the other side of the road: it seemed that Blackgang Chine was losing its rural charm and becoming as commercialised as Godshill. But I visited the Chine again a few years ago and was glad to see that, although the character has inevitably changed, the restricted space has been used imaginatively.

I do not know if the point will ever be reached when the Dabells give up the fight. Not only is the area of their operations threatened, but access to their property is in jeopardy too. The last time I went to the Island I was astonished to find that the road into Blackgang had slipped over the cliff together with a sizeable chunk of Chine and, apparently, the house which used to be Miss Pinnock's. This means that the road through the hamlet has now been severed on each side of it. The other side was cut by the 1928 landslip which made necessary the building of a new road to Niton. It is fortunate that a few years ago a spur from this bypass road was made to provide better access for coaches to the Blackgang Chine car park. This is now the only way in.

Until it eventually becomes softened with vegetation (and this may take several decades) a landslip presents a moonscape appearance of broken up-ended rock, eerie and fascinating. The site of the big 1928 landslide was still wild, frightening, and fun ten years later. It was a world of its own, with miniature forests and fields, and a shudderingly deep lake. One could scramble down to the shore, the most southerly point of the Island – Rocken End – where the feeling was of the utmost remoteness.

Perched on the rim at the end of the broken road was Southview, a substantial house belonging to Sir Frederick Eley of shotgun cartridge fame. Then it was, with other houses, cut off from Blackgang by what we called the "Little Landslide", but a rough track was made across the broken road. Southview is still there, but now further landslides have destroyed all the other houses, and the road is a largely unmetalled track padlocked against all cars except those for Southview. Not surprisingly, the house and its grounds make an ideal nudist camp.

It was quite a walk to the landslip from Chale, and we boys appreciated a spring of drinking water which we found at the side of the road just before reaching Southview. Out of the wall came a spout, to which a metal mug was thoughtfully attached by a chain. Around the spout was a Shakespearian text which read

> The water nectar and the rocks pure gold
> *Two gentlemen of Verona Act 2 Scene 4*

On the bank above was a small classical monument. This has now disappeared, and, sadly, the lead around the spout has been partly stripped away so that the text can no longer be deciphered.

What an incident-packed youth, one may think. But the memory selects the interesting parts and tends to forget the times of boredom. Not infrequently we did not know what to do with ourselves: our circumstances and our geography meant that we had a restricted range of activities, a restricted circle of friends and a restricted number of places to visit. What shall we do? Where shall we go today? were questions often posed. In our teens, cycling out to have beans on toast in a modest teashop in Ventnor gave us something to do, but if Ventnor one week, where the next?

One of our small group of friends was Cecil Brown, also known as Baker from the occupation of his father. He would play with us on the cliffs or at The Steppes, but he would become anxious to return home when it neared the time for his mid-day meal. He would say (standard English) "I shall have to be going, Titch." (I was occasionally called this.) "I will see you this afternoon." In Isle of Wight speech this would become (believe it or not) *Shlaft'begorn, Titch. Seeyasaffernewn.* When he did not wish to commit himself to a definite time of return (perhaps because he was getting fed up with my company) the variant would be "I will see you about Wednesday" (*Seeya bout Wensdee*).

Another memory of Cecil is at Ryde Esplanade, where the public conveniences included a long line of some two dozen cubicles. Cecil went dancing down the row, singing out "Vacant! Vacant! Vacant! Vacant! . . ." until, inevitably, ". . . Oooh!" when he came to one reading 'Engaged', with embarrassed feet visible at the bottom. And one day I clouted poor Cecil with a golf club. Even though it was only a backswing, not a full-force drive, a sheet of blood was flowing down Cecil's forehead and dripping off his nose. Sensibly he caught the vital fluid in his cupped hands and drank it.

Ted and I used to call on another friend, Leslie Eede, because he was much too tired to call on us. We were certainly no larks in the morning, and so it could well be eleven o'clock before we arrived at the Eede household a mile or so away. Without fail his mother would greet us with "Leslie's not up yet". This was spoken in a high-pitched, wet voice reminiscent of the *Monty Python* female impersonations, and was incorporated into our family's stock of catchphrases. Leslie would be seen in a window in his pyjamas reading a lurid American comic. Yes, his mother was over-indulgent. We would make our den in the pigsty in the garden – quite clean because there had been no pigs there for years – and Mrs Eede would bring us a tray of tea, bending down to insert it through the pigs' exit hole into the dark interior.

Leslie had a great passion for the internal combustion engine. We retrieved the wreck of a motorcycle from the dump and refurbished it, my task as the youngest member of the group being to polish the petrol tank. Eventually it was ready for the road and we filled it up with paraffin, petrol being too expensive. Yes, it started, and with Leslie up did proceed for a few yards down the Military Road outside the Eede's house. But then it was slowly but comprehensively enveloped in sheets of yellow flame, closing that particular engineering chapter. Leslie's motor obsession persisted, however. One of his first jobs on leaving school was driving a grocery delivery van, and he made a point of pushing it to its limit like a racing car. He could get only 55mph out of her, but with rough roads and inadequate suspension that would be enough to break a few sugar bags.

Edward "Monkey" Roberts was also the only child of over-protective parents, a fact symbolised for us by his habit of wearing his socks pulled up over his knees. Not surprisingly he was baited by the rest of us. "Sissy! Diddy Den!" we would call out, and he would always rise to the bait, his fury making us double our taunts so that we could see more fun. At home Edward lived in a world of conservative adults and did not fit in with a community of children. He favoured horses over tractors and cars – "nasty smelly things" – and was impervious to our response that horses had their distinctive smell too. He saw and admired the *gravitas* in older members of his family, and his ambition in life was to reach forty years of age as soon as possible. In the fullness of time he made it and looked sixty. Now he really is sixty, and his appearance is so venerable and eccentric that tourists can buy a picture postcard of him as a local rustic character. (Island Images series No.VV 009, photograph by Jeremy Wynne, 1988.)

By contrast with Edward, my youthful objective was to be eighteen years old and to be called Vic Cheap. When I did achieve that age it was time to leave home (still as Peter New) and one mark of my adulthood was the realisation that I need never eat another cabbage in my life. At the same time I thankfully threw off my mother's injunction to "eat bread with it", a rule which seemed to take the fun out of eating. My attitude is unchanged today. My dislike of pizzas springs from the necessity of munching through all that dough which comes with the goodies.

What of the other lads and lasses of the village? The female sex was represented by Hilda Bull and Sylvia

Whittington, always thought of as a pair for some reason, and Ruth Keen of the very blonde hair, a bit rare for an Island girl. Two oddly named male contemporaries were "Kipper" (Clifford) Osman, and David Death, the latter eschewing any euphemism such as De'Ath or the pronunciation 'Deeth'. We did feel a little shiver when we passed his cottage at Presford, on the road to Shorwell. The success story was that of Roy Sheath, who built up a garage business from nothing, in his early years operating in his father's barn. Against this story of admirable enterprise I must set a black mark on his record. It was he who viciously hurled stones at my toy motor boat on the lake at Rocken End until it sank in several fathoms.

Stan Levoir lived at the coastguard cottages at Blackgang: his surname probably indicated Channel Islands origin. We were on the shore one day when he indicated his need to defecate. So he entered the water and lowered his bathing trunks. In due course a turd bobbed to the surface, turned into the wind, and sedately drifted down-Channel. I was horrified. I felt that this single Act had polluted the seas of the world, from Murmansk to Mozambique, from Rio to Rangoon. That was before I knew about sewage outfalls.

It was some years later, I think when I lived at Whitecroft, that I met the most intriguing of my friends, the mysterious Viv Woodward. He lived at Newbridge, beyond Calbourne, a fair cycle ride away. His world of mystery began at a certain spot on the road out from Carisbrooke near Swainston, where trees overhang the road and interlock to form a green tunnel. The story is that no birds sing there: at least that is what coach drivers tell their loads of tourists. In any event we felt a sense of strangeness there.

Viv was interesting in that he was frequently in poor health with quite unspecific ailments, but although he missed a lot of school he made up for it with lots of native intelligence. Even the meals at the Woodward household were odd: either there was no pudding or there was pudding but no main course. (Perhaps they were very poor. Perhaps this was the reason for Viv's poor health.) The final peculiarity was his parentage although we were only half aware of any query at the time. There was no man about the house, only his mother and grandmother. Grandma volunteered the unsolicited information that Viv's father was a sailor killed at sea. This may have been true, but I did note that a visiting tradesman pointedly addressed Viv's mother as *Miss* Woodward. In those days it was important to get the note of censure in.

Viv's main disciple was the silent and acquiescent Denzil Humphreys: he did not have a wide circle of friends, but in his limited and somewhat overheated world he was leader. I too was content to follow even though I had (with Ted) been accustomed to being top dog in previous groups. Viv had an even greater obsession with aircraft than we had, and he spent long hours in model making, making use of his absences from school with his vague and not too serious illnesses. He made 1/72 scale models with a fretsaw and by whittling with a knife, without any kit or instructions, and with a skill we could not match, although we tried enough.

Viv surprised us when he showed what seemed to us to be a quite uncharacteristic interest in a girl, but such a strange and emotional feeling could be expressed only through the safe medium of aircraft. There was a busty young contemporary at school named Lorna Piper who was referred to by Viv and Denzil as the Beaufighter. No-one said, but I gathered that the reason was that the Beaufighter was an aircraft with two large radial engines protruding well in front of the nose. The fact that the engines were Bristols had nothing to do with it, because cockney rhyming slang was quite unknown to us.

We have so far made no mention of sports, and for the good reason that I was hopeless at them. Ball games were out after my initiation in cricket at Scouts, where youths twice my age and size hurled a hard ball at me. I did play tennis from time to time, but invariably took the skin off the base of my index finger. So I thought the least skilful sport I could take up at school was running, and yes, I did come in third in the school mile, but there were only four in the race. One useful ploy when I was in the sixth form was to run the cross-country with the second formers, ostensibly to keep an eye on their welfare . . . At university the opportunities for many sports opened up before me, and I happily settled for coxing the college boat. Bellowing at great oafs (oaves?) to pull me along faster seemed a very sensible sport to me

CHAPTER SIX

Chale

The Irish term is a 'soft' day, but we call it 'Chale weather' when the air is damp – just raining perhaps – and the temperature is mild. Probably Chale had more than its fair share of moisture from the frequent sea mists rolling in over the high cliffs. With the mists came the mournful and penetrating note of the foghorn at St Catherine's lighthouse, two miles away.

The centre of Chale is the three-way road junction by the church. To the south-east you climbed Blythe Shute (Shute or Chute means hill) on which we lived, but after a few yards a turn to the right took you out towards the Terrace, the cliff, and the dump. Continuing up Blythe Shute the Baptist Church was passed on the right, and soon on the left was seen the house adjoining our field, the bungalow of Miss Puckle and Miss Brooke-Alder, who owe their place in my memory solely to their persistent calling for Sandy, their cat, in the cool Chale dusk. On past the Steppes to the top of the hill with Sheep Lane on the left (briefly the home of Grandfather Gold) and a big house called Stonehenge on the right.

Just opposite Stonehenge was a bungalow which belonged to a somewhat bad-tempered farmer called

90

Mortimer. He was important to us mainly because of the fantasy we built up around his name. At the time our cinema diet was made up of American films set in smart New York apartments and concerning gangsters and shady businessmen. So we would swagger about, nasally drawling out of the corner of our mouths, "I'm not going to sign that contract, Mortimer . . ." We didn't take these films seriously, though. Instead of pointing a mock gun at our friends and saying in best hoodlum fashion, "Moving an inch will be signing your death warrant", we adapted to "Moving three feet will be signing your dog licence".

Fifty yards or so after Mortimer's bungalow was a grassy triangle forming a road junction. If you went straight on you would be in Blackgang, although nowadays the road is severed by a recent landslide. The left turn is the New Road to Niton, replacing that swept away by the 1928 landslide. A little way up this road the first wartime bomb on the Isle of Wight fell. The sole casualty was one rabbit. For many years a roadside stile bore perforations from the shrapnel.

The road leading the other way from Chale Church, to the north-west, was the Military Road which ran all the way along the coast to Freshwater. It had this name because it was built by German prisoners of war in the First World War. Some of the original fencing still survives: the hollow metal posts are capped by little cast replicas of soldiers' helmets. When we achieved the age of motorbikes we appreciated the Military Road, because it was so straight and little used that it was eminently suited for speed trials. Our friend Leslie Eede, that obsessive for the internal combustion engine, was fortunate in living on this road.

But before we get to the Edes' house on the Military Road we pass two small farms built at the same time as the Steppes by the County Council for rent to tenant farmers. The houses were as graceless as ours, but the acreage attached was much more: they were farms, ours was a smallholding. Opposite the second of these was a new cottage with the name of Erewebe (it still has that name today). The owners, having a facetious turn of mind, intended it to be pronounced 'Ere we be, but a passer by was heard to observe, "Air Weeb, what a lovely name!".

Down the hill from Erewebe and you come to Walpan Cottages, a semi detached pair shared by the Eedes and Bert Salter. Bert has a place in the gardeners' Valhalla by reason of the quality of the onions he grew, nurtured, it is said, by copious urination. It was to be expected that Bert Salter would carry off the top prizes at all the village shows: if he did not, it was a sign that the Stable Order of Things was crumbling. Each village on the Island had its annual horticultural show, apart from the bigger farming event in Newport. Normally scruffy peasants would be seen in their Sunday best, viewing the exhibits of impossibly long straight carrots and grotesquely huge marrows, whilst their wives would be clucking over the Victoria sponge competition. The smell of trampled grass brings on instant nostalgia.

A little further on were three 'chines' or gullies in the cliff, Ladder Chine, Walpan Chine, and Whale Chine. In my time the first of these offered the official way down to the shore via its hazardous paths and flights of rickety wooden steps. Pop noticed that the spacing of the lettering on the signpost to it on the road was defective, so we always called Ladder Chine *Tothe Shore*. At its top was a strange bowl scooped out in the sandstone by the gyrating wind, with an upstanding core left in the middle. Eventually the effort of repairing the paths and long flights of wooden stairs in face of winter gales and minor landslips became too much, and the route to the sea became Whale Chine, which then faced similar problems.

The third road at Chale church came in from the north, from Chale Green, Chillerton, and Newport. Most of the village activity was concentrated in the quarter-mile between the church and the top of the hill called Kinghall. When I think about the strong sense of place the Island exerts over me, I mull over the example the road towards Chale Green affords of how local names are given to seemingly insignificant stretches which are within shouting reach of each other and in no way distinctive. Thus beyond Kinghall one encounters in turn Yards Hollow, Yards, Fulford, Bramstone, Gotten, and Chapel Corner – all in about a mile. I have no doubt that all the countryside one dashes through in the car *en route* from A to B is equally intensively known and named. Every kink in the hedge, every gate off its hinges, every crumbling barn may be part of some child's history. One man's boring field is another man's loved homeland.

At Chapel Corner one can turn left into Newman (Pop called it Human) Lane which leads towards Pyle and Atherfield, but if you carry straight on you will reach Chale Green, a little village on its own. Before we get there we pass a grassy bank on the left on which in my time were displayed a series of religious texts produced by an organisation known as the Wayside Pulpit. I find it difficult to understand the mechanism whereby one's life is improved by the bald typographic assertion GOD IS LOVE, but I suppose that the mere repetition of the name of the product keeps it in the public eye. Like 'You can be sure of Shell'.

At Chale Green the single shop was run by John Brown, who in his rapid nervous speech designated himself John-Brown-Chale-Green. He was also chapel preacher, county councillor and principal resident. His shop sold everything from foodstuffs to fuel. He would be dispensing petrol at the pump outside, then with a quick wipe of his hands on his apron he would dash back into the shop to cut a few slices of ham for a waiting housewife. He regularly preached at the Wesleyan church at Chapel Corner, and it is said that, seeing one of his customers in the congregation, he would break off from the Word of God to cry out, "I'll send your meat up on Friday Missus Downer!"

Turn left at Chale Green and you follow the bus route to Newport via Chillerton and Whitecroft. Turn right and you pass North Grounds Farm, the home of WAJ ("Wadge") Brown, a large freckled lad who went to the Newport Grammar School. Further on was another farm, which I see from the map is officially named South Side Farm, but we always called it Shitstink. (They kept pigs.) When cycling by we would shout over the wall, "Keep yer stink to yerself!" A mile beyond you will come to Leechmore Corner, which any self-respecting Islander would pronounce *Lashmeer Corner*.

I wonder why the expression is always "I am going *down* to Chale Green"? Never *up*, *over*, or *across*. The reason has no reference to compass direction (rather the reverse – Chale Green is to the north) and has little to do with going downhill. Admittedly one does go *up* to Blackgang and *over* to Niton, because the first is up a hill and the second over the downs. But why *over* to Shorwell (where no downs intervene), *in* to Newport, and *out* to Freshwater? Barbara, as a stranger to the Island, regularly gets these prepositions wrong because there is no logical rule to follow. It is exactly like learning French nouns. To us there is an even chance of saying 'le' when it should be 'la' but natives absorb the right gender with their mother's milk.

But back to Chale proper. Halfway between Kinghall and Chale Church is the Clarendon Hotel, named after one of the many ships wrecked in Chale Bay. At least, I always knew it as the Clarendon, but now it is also using its previous name of The Wight Mouse Inn. It was owned by the Roberts family, headed by old Tom Roberts, a whiskered patriarch who kept a landau in the yard and who thought of himself as the village squire. One of his sons was Ridley Roberts who ran the Clarendon bar, and who was rather a fast young man for Chale, so much so that he upped and left for Bournemouth, or some other unlikely place on the mainland. That left the other son, Henry, who felt that his lot was to stay put and take on the mantle of neo-squire, even though the Clarendon passed out of the family and Henry was left as a very small-time farmer.

When war was approaching we were issued with gas

masks and some official came out to tell us about their use. He emphasised that to demist the eyepiece one should use *toilet* not laundry soap, but despite the clarity of this instruction Henry Roberts had to say his piece, if only to mark his presence as the senior man in the village. So he came out with "Ordinary yellow soap won't do, I suppose?" (*Ornery yellaw soap wun do, spwuz?*) which seemed to indicate that Henry washed himself with the original Sunlight.

As a dairy farmer in a very small way of business, Henry would himself deliver our milk in the mornings from his milk-cart – a churn on wheels. (This must have been when our goats failed to deliver the goods.) We boys knew when he had arrived, not only from the clanging and slopping of the polished brass measuring ladles, but from his invariable remark, "It is going to rain!" (*Gunna rain!*). Of course, given Chale weather, he was usually right. In any event we gained another catchphrase which survives to this day: indeed nowadays when I look out at the lowering skies I merely remark to Barbara "Henry Roberts".

Opposite the Clarendon is Chale School. When I started there the staff consisted of the two Misses Martin and Miss Nicholas who looked after the infants. Later Miss Loosemore became headmistress. I don't remember much of the happenings at Chale School, except that I was thrown out of the country dancing class because of flat feet, an ailment which I had assumed. Dancing seemed cissy to me. One wild night there was a shipwreck at Blackgang – my father had been out with a breeches buoy rescue team – and at school next morning we sang *For those in peril on the sea*, a fat lot of use so long after the event.

A number of ships came to grief along the southwest coast of the Island when I was a boy. A rather unlikely explanation was that eastbound vessels mistook the Needles lighthouse for St Catherines and so turned into the cliffs instead of rounding the eastern side of the Island to enter Spithead. This particular wreck was the *Luigi Accame* which remained stuck fast by the bows for some months, despite efforts to lighten her by jettisoning her cargo of iron ore, staining the sea red. After several attempts and a number of parted hawsers she was eventually pulled off to limp elsewhere for repair. Another ship rammed the cliffs just beyond Blackgang Chine, and one could look down on her vertically from the road above. For some reason I found it surprising that I could distinguish the individual planks of her decking.

I still have in my possession two certificates I gained when I was at Chale School. One, which is now proudly framed, is dated 18th June 1937 and records my proficiency in Religious Knowledge. It is signed by Miss Loosemore, also the Rector, Charles Flavell Blood, and the Bishop, Frank Portsmouth. The other certificate was awarded a year earlier by the Band of Hope for "excellence in reporting a lecture . . . on Alcohol and the Human Body". That talk still sticks in my mind because of the powerful effect of the visual aid the speaker used. A coloured fluid was poured into a test-tube containing a colourless liquid, simulating the absorption of alcohol into the bloodstream. The colour disappeared. Then more and more was added until the test-tube was filled with irremovable colour. Addiction and damage to health was irreversible. The method was hokum, but the message was sound and clear.

I think it was while I was at Chale School that I had the pleasure of being examined by the School Medical Officer. Doctor Fairley was the epitome of the taciturn Scot, for during the whole time he was peering, weighing, and prodding he uttered only two words to me. Yet, incredibly, when I muse over the occasion after the lapse of half a century I must conclude that he was prolix: he could have cut his verbiage down by 100% and conveyed his message with just one word. He could have said just "Strip!" instead of "Strip, boy!".

Further down towards the top of Kinghall was the Scouts' Hall. I had an ambition to join the Scouts long before I was of the proper age, but there was no cub pack. I was particularly narked that I could not be in the Scouts in 1935 because that was the year of the Silver Jubilee of King George V and the Scouts were entrusted with the building, guarding, and lighting of a gigantic bonfire on the downs. So I made myself an honorary Scout, by dressing up more or less appropriately (a large duster was pressed into use as a kerchief) and tagging on behind the troup, and I was accepted as a kind of mascot. The next similar jollification was only two years later; the coronation of King George VI, and by this time I was old enough to join, so I had the privilege of sleeping in a leaky tent on the downs to guard the bonfire.

The Scouts had an annual camp at Binstead, near Ryde, on a site we had used for years and which no doubt had been negotiated for us by our previous Scoutmaster, Mr Cook. His widow still lived at Binstead and annually embarrassed us by providing us with a ready-cooked roast joint on the Sunday. Most un-Scout-like. But back at Chale we were real Scouts, spending most of our time on the cliffs "scouting" in the original sense – stalking one another and camouflaging ourselves in the bracken. My enjoyment was always tempered by my fear of stepping on an adder. Sometimes we played cricket, sometimes we tied knots, and sometimes we did maintenance jobs on the Scouts' Hall, but we never worked for Scout badges. Badges were out, on the say-so of the late Mr Cook who founded our troop. Perhaps he had a genuine moral objection to competition; perhaps the calibre of teachers and taught was such that he wished to save face.

Later we were to learn, to our cost, a practical application of the stalking technique. At the corner by the church, a wooden seat had been set up to mark the 1937 coronation. The coronation seat became a meeting place for pubescent boys and girls, and it was a matter of bravado to push the conversation into more and more daring, not to say dirty, areas. One day my parents had a mis-spelt letter from the excellent Ray Barton, our Scoutmaster. He had crept through the long grass and nettles behind the coronation seat and had overheard our not-so-sweet nothings which he now reported. He had upheld a moral principle and had demonstrated a practical skill, but doubtless his knees were sore.

When France fell in 1940 and there was a fear of invasion, the LDV (Local Defence Volunteers – later called the Home Guard) was formed. Ted was just old enough to join the village platoon, together with Pop. At first there were no uniforms, so armbands had to suffice, and the rifles issued were of a non-standard .300 calibre.

Dad's Army was luxuriously appointed by comparison. I now appreciate the humour of the army officer who devised some manoeuvres for the LDV and named them Exercise Cyclops; yes, it certainly was a one-eyed outfit. J.B. Priestley, the writer, lived at Billingham Manor, between Chale and Chillerton, and in his celebrated wartime broadcasts he would describe his local Home Guard unit. These were people we knew.

Pop did once fire his .300 Home Guard rifle at a German. One day some German 'planes were flying very low over our field: I think they were Junkers 87s, but they were machine-gunning, not dive-bombing. Pop, Ted, and I took shelter in our goats' shed at the top of the hill. After a time Pop ventured his head round the door and took a pot-shot. This was immediately followed by a burst of machine-gun fire. We could not be sure that this was retaliation, but he at once gave up the unequal contest and settled for continued shelter with our capric friends.

Most of the commerce of the village was in the hands of the three brothers Brown. One, sporting the fine name of Trelawny, managed the shop, while Hector and Maurice ran the bakery. Maurice, our friend Cecil's father, delivered the bread, even though any human contact seemed painful for him. He was afflicted with such an extreme nervous disposition that when in conversation his eyes would remain tightly closed. Perhaps his troubles stemmed from the burden his wife was to him.

Myrtle Brown was *huge*. When she got into a crowded bus two gents kindly got up for her but even so there was much overhang of massive buttock. Naturally, with all that weight to haul around she was not too active about the house, and the washing up accumulated in her big sink until, every month or so, Maurice initiated a *blitz*. Like my mother, Myrtle was mad keen on whist. Once they both attended a morning whist drive at which Myrtle won a chicken. They met again at another drive the same evening, where Myrtle greeted Armagh with "I did enjoy that chicken . . ." Myrtle is a pretty name, but for me it has the gross imprint of Mrs Brown on it.

Trelawny (Cecil's "Uncle Tawny") ran his shop with great efficiency and with courtesy bordering on the obsequious. Everything was ship-shape and his goods were of excellent quality. Not only did he buy the best Cheddar cheese but he stored it properly on a cool slab, never in a refrigerator. But Trelawny was too pricey for us, so we had our groceries delivered from the Co-op in Newport. Alas! Ted and I had the reprehensible habit of opening the parcel and picking at the contents. On one occasion we had, in Armagh's absence, gorged ourselves on dried apricots but when mother returned she discovered that the parcel was for one Mrs White, not us. Only a quick dash to Trelawny to make up the missing weight saved the day. I don't think Mrs White ever suspected, but her dried apricots were "a damn close-run thing" as the Duke of Wellington said in a very different context.

We knew little about Miss Cheek because she kept herself to herself, but she was a pillar of the chapel and puritanical to the point where she must have considered that every pleasure was, by definition, a sin, and the normal commerce of life an obscenity. It was this lady who featured in a little ditty Pop adapted from the Irving

Berlin song of the time:

> Oh! I like to go a-fishing
> In a river or a creek
> But I don't enjoy it half as much
> As dancing with Miss Cheek

Then Pop saw the danger. He summoned his sons and solemnly enjoined us, on pain of a most uncharacteristic thrashing, not to utter the corrupted version outside the house lest sound of it should reach Miss Cheek or her chapel circle.

Not far from Miss Cheek lived the Misses Plumbley. Again, we did not know much about them but they were clearly of a conservative and rigid nature. We saw them only when they were slowly and sedately cycling past, and it was their bicycles which intrigued us so. They were of the upright roadster type complete with wicker basket and dress-guard of cords radiating round the rear wheel. We wondered what would happen if these prim ladies ever needed to mend a puncture, raise the handlebars, or tighten the chain. From these speculations evolved the concept of the Plumbley Non-Adjustable Bicycle, which would have suited their needs. Heights and adjustments would be made once and for all at the factory and solid tyres would eliminate risk of punctures.

Between Miss Cheek and the Misses Plumbley was the Baptist chapel. Although we subscribed to the Church of England Ted and I were regular visitors to the chapel because of the free slide shows. Not that the content was rivetting – views of the Holy Land – but it passed a wet evening and there was fun to be had in observing the minister, the Reverend Stephen Jarvis, and his mishaps. The evening was punctuated with hymns, the words of which were lettered on a special slide with some religious pictorial embellishment. We were quite delighted when Christ on the cross flashed on to the screen upside down. If all was well the Rev Jarvis would drone out the first verse in his nasal voice, follow it by "Shall we rise, friends?", and so we would break into singing, accompanied on the harmonium by Herbert, Stephen's son. I have never seen such a sinful looking man, swarthy, hirsute and beetle-browed. *Easy on the vox humana, Herbert.*

In those days projectors were called "magic lanterns" and the light source was probably acetylene, so they were fierce and unpredictable monsters. Sooner or later the operator would burn himself, and when we heard a sharp, hissing intake of breath we knew that Stephen had done just that. Now one would expect that anyone in these circumstances would hop about, sucking his fingers and blaspheming profusely. Poor Stephen Jarvis. As a minister all he could do was utter a heartfelt "Oh dear! Its getting hot!" Another catchphrase (spoken in a nasal voice) joined our list.

But we were committed to the Church of England, not through any religious conviction but in response to family and social pressures. We would certainly have preferred to be playing down the dump rather than singing in the choir, and to this day, long after the end of any connection with the church, I feel a sense of guilt for my absence whenever I hear church bells.

Until 1933 Chale had a much loved rector, the

Reverend Geoffrey Heald. He was of a Low Church persuasion which suited the village fine, but it was odd because the living was in the gift of Keble College Oxford, which could not be more High Church. So when the good Rev Heald departed, we were sent a succession of unacceptable Anglo-Catholics, culminating in the arrival of the Reverend Charles Flavell Blood. He was charismatic, and had all the women of the village in a flutter, but he was uncompromisingly a High Churchman. Soon we found that the familiar blue Hymns Ancient and Modern was replaced by the up-church green English Hymnal, and we were induced to learn strange new hymns.

The Rector asked me – perhaps in a confirmation class – how I would describe the church, and I replied "Protestant". His face suffused with eponymous blood, and for a moment he was silent with shock, but when he recovered he thundered that we belonged to the Holy Catholic Church, which was news to me. His most memorable dictum was "If I can't have incense I shall smoke a cigarette." Very funny, but the rector split the village. Hordes left to worship at other denominations, leaving only a dwindling band around the rector. One who remained loyal was Mr Stowell, a big man who sang bass in the choir. (Astonishingly he was stung by a bee and died.) The religious schism in the village was never fully repaired even though the Reverend Charles Flavell Blood eventually left, perhaps as a result of a delegation a number of village elders made to the bishop, who, as we have seen, had the approachable name of Frank Portsmouth.

I have long since left the church, but being a choirboy

at Chale for so many years has left its indelible mark: the church bells still reprove me and the hymn tunes are laden with nostalgia. Although the words of hymns are often inane and of very dubious theology and the rhymes are frequently contrived, the phraseology of the Book of Common Prayer is superb. Some words are woven into my vocabulary, and are trotted out when appropriate, such as "a happy issue out of all our afflictions". And I marvel at the quality of the poetic prose in, for example, the prayer which runs

> . . . to give and not to count the cost, to fight and not to heed the wounds . . .

and concludes with the overflowing cadence of

> To labour and not to ask for any reward, save that of knowing that we do Thy will.

or the prayer which goes

> . . . the busy world is hushed and the fever of life is over . . .

and ends

> . . . and peace at the last.

CHAPTER SEVEN

Newport Tec

The Number 10 bus ran through Chale on its way from Newport to Ventnor, and although we were nearer to Ventnor, we thought of Newport as our home town. It was bigger, it was where the family did its shopping, and where we boys went to secondary school.

The evolution of a town is fascinating. I have several views down Newport High Street from St James's Square. The earliest is an 1822 engraving by George Brannon, another is a Francis Frith photograph of 1892, and I have myself taken photographs from the same viewpoint. Many of the buildings are the same throughout, but the Victorians added a clock tower to the classical Town Hall, and a lamp standard-cum-fountain was transformed into a statue of Queen Victoria, commemorating her Diamond Jubilee of 1897.

But of course there is change over the timespan of my own memory: buildings are demolished and others built, shops change hands. Pollard and Ramage, the chemists, is no longer at the junction where High Street and Pyle Street eventually converge at "top of town" but I still half expect to see it there. Bekens, another chemist's shop, has departed from St James's Square; this was a branch of

Bekens of Cowes, famed for photographing yachts more than for any pharmaceutical prowess. The Victory Cleaners still survives, as does Frank E Whitcher, the Wight Man's Clothier. Mr Whitcher was very fortunate during the war, because surrounding property was bombed flat, and his shop was left standing, as isolated as a single incisor in a toothless mouth. He eventually moved elsewhere in Newport, leaving an unencumbered site for redevelopment as the new bus station.

In my time the bus station was in St James's Square and I think I remember the cattle market being held there too. The major bus company was the Southern Vectis (Vectis was the Roman name for the Isle of Wight) Omnibus Company, but there were others operating single routes, such as Enterprise to Sandown and Shotters to Shorwell and Brighstone. They were all eventually bought up. Island passengers travelling home from work, school, or shopping had a long-standing grievance in summer that they were crowded off the buses by the flocks of tourists, and attempts to overcome the problem included picking up Islanders at bus stops unknown to the visitors.

My mother's moan was not only that the fares went up in summer to exploit the visitors, but that they did not come down again to the same extent in winter. Islanders have an ambivalent attitude to the hordes of people who fill the island in summer. On the one hand the influx contributes importantly to the economy, and I am sure that holiday-makers are not fleeced unduly and that most contacts are friendly. But on the other hand we boys at least could not but be amused by our guests' ignorance of the Island and its ways, their unfamiliar speech, and their insistence on wearing beach clothes regardless of the weather. The dialect books will tell you that Islanders refer to those from over the water as 'overners', but I have never heard the term used. My nieces, who do holiday work in Godshill tearooms, call their customers 'grockles' (not to their face), but this is at best a humorous revival of a dialect word rather than normal Island speech.

All the events of Newport, indeed of the Island, were recorded in the local newspaper, whose full name was *The Isle of Wight County Press and South of England Reporter with which is incorporated The Isle of Wight Express*. When I went to university, and after, my mother regularly sent me the current CP with her letters. I always thanked her, employing the full title of the journal. Whilst the record of the meetings of Ningwood and Shalfleet Women's Institute were not of earth-shattering importance, local events impinge on our lives more than do most goings-on in faraway countries. I always looked out for the little religious pieces put in the paper by Isaac Crutcher, who regularly added the puzzling initials AEPSA after his name. We thought that this might be some dubious American degree, but all was made clear when, in one issue, he spelled out his qualifications in full. They were 'Author Evangelist Preacher and Spiritual Adviser'.

The grizzled and taciturn Mr Stevens was the County Press's photographer: he could be depended upon to put in an appearance at all important Island goings-on, such as the County Show, always held at a field in Newport called Nine Acres. This was before the days of the 35mm camera. Stevens would be encumbered with a leather box in which he housed his Speed Graphic or Graflex or whatever model his solidly made press camera was. The home of the County Press is still 29 High Street.

Just opposite the County Press offices you will find a ladies' hairdresser with the unexceptional name of Michael Jon. In my boyhood the same trade was carried on at these premises, but under the laughable name of Maison Biddlecombe. It is difficult to follow the thinking of the proprietor who, while achieving some Gallic *chic* with 'Maison', saw no need to follow suit with 'Biddlecombe', which conjures up a vision of an apple-cheeked Devonian farmers's wife rather than anything to do with sophisticated coiffure. A very similar oddity was in Union Street in Ryde, where one could find another ladies' hairdresser, this time Maison Hackshaw. The stationers and newsagents next to Newport Post Office could not help having the name Greengrass, but given the popularity at the time of the Ink Spots we could not resist

Why do you whisper 'Greengrass' –
That little stationers in Post Office Lane?
Whispering grass...

No-one who knew Newport in my time could be unaware of Westmores. It was partly a working class tea room in that there were a few tables at which one could perch uncomfortably and have a cup of tea while the business of the shop went on, but the fame of the establishment rested on its supreme jam doughnuts. These were produced by a certain Mr Shepherd with a withered arm, who would appear from a back room, tray held aloft to avoid clouting the tea-drinkers, and shoot the contents into a bin against the greasy front window. But those doughnuts . . . hot from the oven, coated in sugar, and with a spurt of scalding red jam inside. Whenever I see a doughnut these days, it is compared with the Westmore's standard: those dreadful things with a hole in the middle just don't enter the competition.

The other Newport – indeed Island – speciality was chiddlings. Not even the most educated person pronounces their name chitterlings, which is how it is spelt. Not to put too fine a point on it, chiddlings are pigs' guts, cleaned (we hope) and boiled. They are plaited for sale in rather pretty patterns, and may be eaten cold or may be fried, when a distinctive and by no means unpleasant aroma arises. It is only when one thinks of the origin of the things that one can read all sorts of nastiness into the smell. Delicious. I believe that chiddlings were on the menu when I introduced Barbara to my parents: she passed the test well – ordeal by chiddlings. The Great Mecca for chiddlings was Scarrotts Lane, a narrow passageway full of slaughterhouses. They have all gone now, centralised somewhere I expect, and in their place is a row of little twee antique shops.

Particular Newport people flit through the mind such as the couple living at Whitcombe, the husband furtive and foxy, the wife with a mouth overfull with teeth. Or the pop-eyed conductor on the Enterprise bus to Sandown. Impossible to overlook was Pester Jackson, the aptly named hawker of suspect fruit. His raucous cry would be "Fresh, fresh ripe, fresh ripe strawberries. Strawberries, strawberries, fresh, fresh ripe strawberries, fresh . . ." and so on. Appropriately enough, he had a monstrous strawberry nose.

If there were roadworks afoot in Newport, you would expect to see Fred Stephens. Fred was harmless, aimiable, but decidedly simple, and he had the habit of attaching himself to gangs of workmen and pretending to be one of the boys. Thus he would be seen wiping the sweat from his brow – as he had learned from his companions – even though all he was carrying was one of those red warning lamps. Folks would taunt him, if only to get his inevitable twisted response. "You're daft Fred!" they would call out, and he would reply, not quite saying what he intended, "So you are! So you are too!". The story of Fred's downfall is that a sweet old lady asked him where the Post Office was, and he, thinking this the proper parlance of working men, replied with that well known and coarse catchphrase which is the common response of the vulgar when asked where something is, or where it should be put. Apparently the sweet soul was an influential visitor, and she had a quiet word with the Borough Surveyor.

So when Ted and I took the revolutionary step of passing the scholarship examination (Ted was the first to manage this from Chale since 1908) we went to school at the institution popularly known as "the Tec" from its previous existence as a technical institute. It was at the top of Upper St James's Street (Nodehill) at the junction with Medina Avenue and Trafalgar Road, next door to the County Seely Library and within earshot of the whine of Morey's sawmills. This was one of the two county secondary schools on the Island, and was the nearer to Chale, the other one being at Sandown. I was in receipt of a maintenance grant – I don't know how much it amounted to, but I gather that such grants were discretionary and rare.

Those who did not pass the scholarship exam stayed at their elementary school until the school leaving age – unless their parents had the funds to send them to a fee-paying establishment. The Newport example was the Newport Grammar School, whose main claim to fame was that Charles the First had stayed there briefly before his imprisonment in Carisbrooke Castle. The Grammar School was, in contrast to the Tec, non-selective: the only criterion for entry was the ability to pay. Thus it was largely populated by the offspring of affluent farmers who valued the social cachet, or by those unable to make it to the Tec.

I had a little contact with some of the Grammar School boys at the Literary Society in Quay Street (in practice a snooker hall as far as we were concerned), but they were rather strange. One of their sports was to 'phone up a local greengrocer in the middle of the night just to disturb him and to have the pleasure of hearing him say "Wapshott Newport!" in his rather wet voice. Although the Grammar School boys would repeat this to themselves and chuckle hugely, I did not, and do not, think the jape very funny.

We went back and forth from the Tec on the bus, and whiled away the time with varied horseplay. Being a little chap I was bundled into the overhead luggage rack, whilst my companions were probably using illicit cigarettes to burn the message on the back of the seats "Mind your head when rising from seat" and change it to something rude. The bus stopped at the top of Blythe Shute, well beyond our house, so I would make a point of slinging out my school satchel as we passed, aiming for the bullseye of hitting our steps.

As I was to find later at university, moving up in the world posed no problems: the difficulty was merely in the relationships with the people I had left behind. There was some resentment – at least initially – amongst the Chale folk over our translation to the Tec, a feeling heightened by the rarity of the event. I soon felt comfortable at the secondary school, both socially and academically. I was fairly able, although probably not very well prepared by Chale School, and the effect was that I alternated between the upper stream of my year and the lower stream of the year above me, thus I cannoned into *The Merchant of Venice* at every turn. I can quote you whole chunks all the way from:

> In sooth I know not why I am so sad
> It wearies me, you say it wearies you...

to:

> ...I'll fear no other thing
> ...as keeping safe Nerissa's ring.

I made friends at school, but many more friendly acquaintances, the distinction being because pupils travelled from half of the island and there was little opportunity of meeting out of school hours. Gordon Philpot came from Cowes – about as far from Chale as it is possible to get. He sat in front of me in class, his huge protuberant ears an irresistible temptation to flick. His friend Desmond Russell also had noteworthy ears – they were always filthy. (I was probably none too pristine myself: I did find a piece of soap in my satchel one day – a hint?)

There were some social activities at school or arranged by school, but they were always limited by the inexorable timetable of buses to get home. Of course, daily morning assembly was a form of social gathering. Immediate nostalgia is brought on when I hear Handel's march from *Scipio*, because this was invariably the tune thumped out on the piano to which we marched out of the school hall, making the splintery oiled-board floor quiver. Another daily social event was the unofficial and quite unnecessary morning snack. Westmores (of the superb jam doughnuts) was too far to reach so went to another cake shop, just down Nodehill. It must have done an excellent trade in special small one-boy sized Coventry cakes: we ate one each, just like a bun.

In my early days at the school our headmaster was the splendid N.A.Y. Yorke-Lodge, remarkable for his name, efficiency, scholarship, and the smallness of his handwriting. He was the successor to the formidable Miss Monk who had been headmistress since 1910 and who was still just in office when Ted joined the school three years before me.

It was Yorke-Lodge who led our school journey to St Briac, near St Malo, in 1938. I was the youngest member of the party, and at twelve I was really too young to gain full benefit. I do not remember much of it, and when revisiting St Briac some forty-five years later I could find nothing I recognised, not even the *Pension Edelweiss* at which we stayed. But the enduring memory is of Yorke-Lodge leading a crocodile of us up the hill from the riverside at Dinan. It was a hot day, the climb was steep, we were going through a poor area – I could see that newspaper had been used as wallpaper. Ragged people sat on doorsteps and it stank a bit. When we sweatily reached the top, even the dapper Yorke-Lodge was glowing a little. Putting a neatly folded handkerchief to his brow he turned round to address us. "How quaint!" he said. As is the way with the best people, Yorke-Lodge soon moved on, to be County Education Officer for Warwickshire, I believe.

Another teacher who went with us to St Briac was Mr Waterson, the maths teacher. For some reason he was always known as Diz, possibly through the declension Waterson, Walt Disney, Disney, Dis. He was famed for his fiery temper, which was played upon by the more courageous of us. Not surprisingly, he could be incensed by our chanting "That man Diz, what a fool he is!", but in some ways he was the architect of his own anger. He never took exercise books in for marking, but checked homework over publicly in class asking how many had five right, how many four, and so on. This was an invitation to us to do no homework and merely to claim a number of correct answers which would not attract attention. But just now and then, his suspicions would be aroused and he would ask to see a book. Incredulous, he would demand to inspect another, and another . . . and all would tell the same story. The series of explosions was both alarming and entertaining.

It would not surprise you to learn that I am no good at maths (that is why people become librarians) but my deficiency was there from Chale School days. Otherwise I was academically an all-rounder, but the failing in maths

115

cut short any hopes of progressing in science. I could carry out experiments with all proper scientific accuracy, but the results would be fouled up because my arithmetic would let me down. This occurred dramatically when I was engaged on determining the heat of a Bunsen burner, which entailed dropping red-hot rivets into a Eureka can filled with water. All done with praiseworthy scientific exactitude, but I achieved the result of 24,000 degrees Centigrade, or four times the heat of the sun. I had multiplied when I should have divided.

Our science teacher was the pleasant and shy Harry Daw

> Oh! Harry Daw is dead and gone
> He's laid out on the floor
> For what he thought was H_2O
> Was H_2SO_4

It fell to Harry to explain the workings of the human body, to his great embarrassment when it came to the elimination of waste products. Sometimes he was played up by lads feigning hiccups and asking "Please Sir, may I go out and get a drink of water?". Harry's rapid and nervous reply came out almost as one word, "No-you-can't-Sit-down-and-hold-your-breath". Above all, I am very grateful to Harry Daw for setting me on the road to photography. He founded a school photographic society with a well equipped darkroom, and he even lent me a camera, which would be a valuable antique nowadays. It was a quarter-plate box plate camera in which a dozen glass plates were stacked vertically to fall down to the horizontal (with a great clang) after exposure. Let us leave Harry anxiously rapping on the darkroom door when he realisèd that a boy and a girl were inside . . . "What are you doing in there?"

Other teachers included Phillip Bagwell, obviously inexperienced, but I was too good or too scared to give him trouble. Forty years later I heard of him again. He was a professor at the Polytechnic of Central London, a historian of some repute. Quite different was the very senior P.W.F. Erith (BA Hons) who had a fine reputation as a teacher and as a major in the army, although we thought him a sarcastic bully, even mildly sadistic. He often imposed extra work on Peter and David Whittle for their incurable waywardness. And when that work was not well enough done, Erith would take great delight in setting yet more, to the accompaniment of an oily smile and *"Non satisfecit,* Whittle!" And one should always distrust anyone who parades the designation 'Hons' – it probably means a third class degree.

If Harry Daw had to explain human anatomy to us, it fell to P.W.F. Erith to lecture us on personal hygiene one day. His embarrassment at the topic made him even more unpleasant than usual. He was anxious that we should dry ourselves properly after washing, and confessed that, hurrying to get to school to teach us, he might slip up in this respect himself – somehow he suggested that it was our fault. He also detailed the areas to which we should pay particular attention in our ablutions ". . . under the armpits, the soles of the feet . . ." and, daring us to snigger, ". . . *around the private parts.*"

Mr Laundy was the specialist in woodwork, and like Mr Waterson, he had a quick temper. He also had the habit of beating you about the ears with the imperfect

117

wooden artefact you had created. Amazingly I once fooled him into thinking I had made a tight joint by jamming two dovetailed pieces together the wrong way round. Laundy would ask a boy to go down to the newsagents at morning break to get him a *Daily Telegraph*, and should the messenger bring the *News Chronicle* by mistake, this would be thrashed about his head to the accompaniment of *"The Daily Telegraph*, you silly muggins!" The term "muggins" and the accent indicated that Mr Laundy came from some vague faraway place in the north of England.

Taffy Davies, of the shining bald head, taught geography, and, being Welsh, singing as well. He also tried unsuccessfully to introduce Rugby. He was firm, fair, and eccentric. He had me out in front of his desk on one occasion, and I wondered if I were to be praised or condemned. He turned me towards the class and proceeded to give them a not unflattering description of me. "This is New. He is a very fine chap . . ." and so on. Eventually the point was made – ". . . but he needs to lose his fountain pen". Another time he was examining the possible reasons for the class's poor performance in a test, eliminating one after the other in a calmly analytical way. All this was building up the tension in the class, and at last the *dénouement* came. "I think I know why results are so bad in this test." (All in a most reasonable voice). "It is because people don't take their books home, and WORK and WORK and WORK". At each WORK he slammed down his desk lid with explosive force: we were shattered.

It is surprising that such a good teacher used the enumerative 'capes and bays' method so much. Actually

118

it was railway stations we were required to memorise, such as those on the Trans-Siberian Railway, running through Omsk and Tomsk and terminating at Vladivostock. The route of another, European, line (Orient Express?) survives in my memory only in the phrase 'skirting the edge of the Ardennes', but I am reminded of the east coast line from London to Edinburgh every time I travel on a British train. The sequence of stations matches exactly the rhythm of the wheels on the rails

Hitchin, Huntington, Peterborough, Grantham, Doncaster, Selby, York . . .

(All these places took on reality a few years later when I travelled up to Durham.) I expect Taffy was a train buff, spending his summers exploring both famous routes and the 'little trains of Wales'. Later he went on to be headmaster of Ryde School, an independent establishment.

French was taught by Miss Winifred J. Damp (Madamoiselle Humide) who sprang (perhaps oozed would be a better word) from a long line of local undertakers. She had been a pupil at our school, left it briefly to get her degree at Southampton, and then returned as a teacher; not a sequence leading to wide comparative views. She was the dullest of French teachers because she was concerned with the minutiae of the grammar to the exclusion of the sweep and meaning of the literature. So in a whole year we would probably get through only a score or so pages of *Columba* or *Captifs dans la montagne* and consequently so little was covered that one gained no idea of the plot. "Win" was

119

not very good at keeping order, either. The boys in Ted's form used to have a session of Extra French when the girls were at singing, at which they learned little French, but indulged in Health Contests whereby points could be scored, one for a fart, five for a pee, right up to a prized fifty for being sick.

A very different kind of French teaching came to the school with the arrival of D.H. Greatwood MA L-ès-L as headmaster. He had a French wife, and I still squirm with embarrassment at Miss Damp's efforts to converse with her. (And to think that Win Damp had the effrontery to tell *me* that I spoke French with an Isle of Wight accent!) Greatwood was short, podgy, and wore a flat working class cap when he cycled to school from his house on Alvington Shute at Carisbrooke. I met him as a French teacher in the sixth form where numbers were small. When the three or four of us filed into his office for our lesson he would greet us with "Eh bien, bien, bien, mes enfants!" to the accompaniment of a liquid noise made by rubbing together his fat little hands. But good old Greatwood: he taught French as literature. I owe to him my knowledge of the French romantic poets – Lamartine, Musset, Vigny, Hugo, Gautier – and the impressive *Le Grand Meaulnes* of Alain-Fournier. His *alter ego* was Flight Lieutenant Greatwood, Officer Commanding 757 Flight Air Training Corps, and on one night a week I was under his command.

CHAPTER EIGHT

Life at the Looney Bin

Tell an Islander that you live at Whitecroft and he will fall about laughing. It is like saying that you reside at Pentonville or Wormwood Scrubs, because Whitecroft, near Gatcombe in the centre of the Island, is the site of the Isle of Wight County Mental Hospital. When we abandoned poultry keeping and left Chale we came to live at Whitecroft Farmhouse, one of the very few houses in the hamlet which had no connection with the hospital.

We had no farm to run; we merely had a delightful, over-large, and somewhat ramshackle house in which to live. There were big floored attics which were empty except for a few wrinkled stored apples, so they provided generous space in which I could wage sea battles between my model ships and those of my friends. One snag of the place was that it was not on mains water, but relied on manual pumping to fill up the cold water tank from a well. It fell to Pop to do most of the work with the semi-rotary pump by the back door, but there was some attempt to use the task as a punishment by imposing penalties of fifty or 100 strokes for some transgression. And it was here where Ted developed his electrical skills and his musical taste. Both found expression in the

121

motley collection of extension loudspeakers to the radio which he set up all round the house. Several were "Strongarms" (see p76) and one was a huge unstable horn which could usually be found hanging by its flex out of an ever-open upstairs window, providing the BBC Home Service for callers at the back door from its position in the gutter above.

In such a large house there was no difficulty in taking a paying guest, so Miss Taylor, the hospital occupational therapist, stayed with us for a time. She was a modern miss; quick, bright and attractive, who combined a genuine interest in us with a proper degree of keeping herself to herself. She cooked her own meals – that was part of the contract, but it would have been awkward if it had not been so, because she was a vegetarian. But she discovered that I had reached my late teens without knowing how to use the telephone: in fact there was no need for the family to incur the expense of a phone at home and no occasion for me to use a public booth had ever occurred. She sought to remedy the defect by instruction, encouragement, and an invitation to ring her at work at any time. I think she was a bit disconcerted when I took her up on her offer. Pop found Miss Taylor disturbing: she was not only lively and attractive, but she had the habit of flitting about the house in short shorts and suntop. It was not Puritan disapproval but simple lust, and Armagh was asked to have a quiet word.

We were tenants of Sir Vere Hobart, who lived in Gatcombe House. We called him Severe Sir Vere with some justification, because he was of the old school of squirearchy, and could not have been more unpleasant, particularly when, only two or three years after we moved in, it suited his purpose to try to get us out. As one of the gentry, he was, of course, unable to pronounce his "r"s, so when he came round on one of his unannounced tours of inspection he would prod with his stick at one or two pieces of paper lying about, vent his wrath, and tell us that litter "bweeds wats". To give more weight to his threats, he would remind us that he was a "magistwate".

Most of the other houses in Whitecroft were part of the hospital complex and were built in the same rude red Hampshire brick. In addition to these houses – for the Medical Superintendent, the Finance Officer and so on – there was a farm, which was largely staffed by patients. Many years later there was a change of policy, whereby patients were not to be used as cheap labour, and whereby hospitals bought in all food rather than producing any themselves. One wonders how the patients occupied themselves when they did not have farm work to do; work which was within their capabilities, which many might expect to do outside hospital, and which probably engendered more self respect than occupational therapy.

We had just changed over the terminology from 'inmates' and 'attendants' to 'patients' and 'nurses'. Some of the long-serving staff were hard and institutionalised, probably not through any motivation of cruelty, but as a protection against becoming too personally involved with a particularly demanding kind of patient. The same phenomenon can be found in all the 'caring' professions, and indeed some people leave them because they cannot be detached enough to survive. Armagh, Pop, and I all worked at the hospital at one time or another, myself for short periods in university vacations. We all felt that it

123

was difficult to tell some of the staff from the patients.

The Medical Superintendent was Dr Charles Davies-Jones, brilliant and eccentric. He was certainly capable of moving upward to greater responsibility and a larger hospital, but doubtless he was content with an agreeable life on the Island. He lived at the hospital, but had a delightful remote retreat (Hoy Cottage) just under the summit of the downs above Chale Green. Possibly a bar to his promotion was his habit of inviting plump young male nurses to camp in his garden at Whitecroft. Part of his duties was to train his staff, and Pop told us that he used the method, which I was to find commonly used in the armed forces, of making facts memorable by lacing them with naughty stories.

The most feared person in the hospital by far was Matron. To say that she was a dragon of the old school would seriously understate the position. No-one would dare cross her and she frequently reduced young nurses to tears. When on duty she was, of course, addressed as Matron, but the moment she went off duty to her quarters in the hospital she insisted on being called Miss Mortlock. She was most strict about this, and I have had a verbal lashing from her for forgetting it. She did once praise me though, albeit indirectly. When I was working in the kitchens a message came from Miss Mortlock thanking whoever it was who sliced up her runner beans so finely. It was me. I felt that the clouds had parted and that a shaft of light had signalled from above that I was in divine favour.

Armagh was never formally trained as a mental nurse, but she offered her services as a V.A.D. (Voluntary

Aid Detachment). On her ward she had, concurrently, three self-styled queens, two Queens of England and one Queen of Sykes. She recounted to us the story of a fellow nurse who was puzzled by not being able to find the source of an extremely nasty smell which was clearly very close to her. A search eventually revealed that a patient had taken a nodule of excrement, rolled it into a ball like plasticine, and popped it under the nurse's shoulder strap.

It was obvious even to the layman that there were broadly two kinds of patient; those with a mental disorder, who might otherwise be very intelligent, and those who were permanently sub-normal in mental ability. As far as I know, the latter did not get, and did not require, treatment; all they wanted was a sheltered environment in which to live, because they could not cope with looking after themselves in the world outside. It was this kind of patient who worked on the farm, and one such was Frank Andrews. Frank would deliver the milk without fail every morning and became so likeable that we gave him a present on his birthday. His response was a child-like "Is that for Frank?"

One bonus of living at Whitecroft was that we had access, without charge, to the tennis courts outside the main entrance of the hospital. (It would have been a bigger bonus had I been able to play tennis effectively rather than just have it as a means to blister my finger). The players would be a mixture of patients and non-patients such as myself. One patient was Alfie, who had heaps of natural ability but no instruction in tennis. He referred to his racket as a bat, held it halfway up the handle and jabbed with it. But he won games.

Another patient was of the 'mental disorder' type, cultured, intelligent, well educated, and obviously coached in the strokes of tennis. He played Alfie, and notwithstanding his text book strokes and beautiful follow-through, he lost again and again and again. At last his excessive politeness broke down, and we were embarrassed to see him prostrate himself in frustration and grovel in front of his persistent victor, muttering "My lord and master . . . I am not worthy . . . your great skill . . ." and other anguished cries of self-abasement.

On the first occasion I worked at the hospital it was for a month or two as a hall porter. The head hall porter, despite the fact that he walked to work every day all the way from Newport, had a considerable paunch, covered by a disreputable uniform waistcoat into which the spilled ash of countless Woodbines was patted. Sometimes I was on night duty, and the vivid memory of that is the pint mug of sweet, strong, orange coloured tea brought to me at dawn by the boiler man. Ugh! I can still taste it!

The main part of the job was to operate the manual telephone switchboard, and at slack times I would have a little chat with the unknown voices on the other end. One beautiful Irish voice was that which softly said "This is Nurse Cass speaking", and I particularly looked forward to a few words with her. One day she appeared before the window of the hall porters' office and announced herself. The appearance and the voice did not match, and my fantasy was shattered.

The next time I wanted temporary employment at the

hospital, there was no vacancy as a hall porter, so I found myself working as a kitchen porter instead. This was the first time I had seen mass catering, and I was disgusted with the lack of care taken and with the petty pilfering which was accepted as legitimate perks. No-one bothered to put in any salt when the potatoes were boiled, or even to take the eyes out after machine peeling. It was like pigs' swill. Cheese was liberally dispensed to kitchen workers as elevenses, far in excess of the ration allocated to the patients on the wards – remember that food rationing was in force. The kitchen was presided over by two cooks; Sid Cassford the senior, and Bert Hambry the junior partner. Both were short tempered, as is the way with cooks. I ventured to voice my complaints to Bert Hambry, and was immediately whipped along to see that ultimate ogre, Matron.

Several patients worked in the kitchen, doing menial jobs of some sort. A regular routine throughout the hospital wards was to count the knives every day in case a patient had murderous or suicidal ideas, and the knives were sharper and more plentiful in the kitchen, so the kitchen helpers were not allowed them at all. One very useful patient was Len Parkin who had a water fetish. He was given the job of rinsing out the huge tea urns as they came back from the wards and this he did with gusto. A gleam would come into his eye and he would thunder the water out of the tap with totally unnecessary force.

Sid Cassford spilled the custard once: he swore, then called out in a firm, clear voice "Albert Bull!". His tone was certainly not cruel, but it had not an atom of warmth in it, and might approximate to that of an unimaginative shepherd calling a working dog. After a few moments

Albert Bull appeared shuffling from the scullery, trailing a broom behind him, around the head of which was draped a wet cloth, so that he left a glistening trail on the floor tiles, like a snail. As he advanced, a stream of invective could be detected, but it was difficult to follow, because, like many mental defectives, Albert had a cleft palate. So to the accompaniment of muffled foul language, the custard was mopped up.

Les Spinks was so trusted that he was – against all the rules – allowed to use a knife. Then, accidentally, he cut himself, which needed a lot of explanation. He is for ever fixed in my memory because he persistently sang a little truncated tune to himself

And when I die, don't bury me

He never completed the line to ". . . bury me at all" so that it could rhyme, as it should, with "Just pickle my bones in alcohol", so the single abbreviated line irritated me more and more. At about the thirty-ninth repetition I could stand no more. Rhyming 'me' with 'TNT' I composed another – very rude – line which put forward an alternative, and explosive, method of disposal of the body. I had to explain it carefully to Les because he did not know what TNT was. Eventually he understood, and when he did, a slow, delighted, and filthy leer spread over his face. He took enormous pleasure in crooning his new couplet softly but audibly when standing behind Matron on her visits of inspection to the kitchen. He was sly enough to know that as a patient he could not be touched.

We were at Whitecroft during the time I went

128

through sixth form, the RAF, and university. Most of my friends in the early part of this period were from school, and as Whitecroft was not as remote as Chale, we could visit one another more easily. My only contemporaries living at Whitecroft were Alan Nelson, whose grandfather was a senior administrator at the hospital, and Eric Prangnell from the hospital farm. Neither went to my school, but the very smallness of our community meant that there was none of the expected resentment at my being at a secondary school.

Eric had a pet dog called Scamp, or Scampy (not Scampi, I think). He would croon to it the following endearment: "Only a little puppers – four and a half (*four-naff*) years old..." Later, when I was at university, it was Eric with whom I had a conversation about poetry, which he had thought consisted entirely of sentimental verse about "nature". I got that special teachers' thrill of imparting an insight to another, and I hope and believe that I avoided condescension.

A school friend very much in my own mould was Rodney Charlesworth. Like me, he had a mad sense of verbal humour. We noticed that the auxiliary policemen of the time (Police War Reserves or PWRs) almost always patrolled the streets in pairs, so we referred to them as though they were pheasants – "a brace of PWRs". If, exceptionally, a single policeman were seen, he would, of course, be designated "half a brace of PWRs".

Between us we produced a fair number of nonsense poems and crazy lyrics to music. For example, when we were studying Australia in geography we produced our own version of *Old folks at home*:

> Way down upon the Murrumbidgee
> In New South Wales
> Way down upon the Murrumbidgee
> Selfridge's annual sales.

We made some sort of political comment from a nonsense song of the time:

> Chicory-chick, cha-la, cha-la
> Viva de Gaulle! Down with Daladier!

And in honour of Mr Dingle Foot MP we adapted *I've got spurs . . .* as follows:

> I've got feet
> That dingle, dangle, dingle . . .

We also invented an adhesive. This came from the tango of the time

> They call him Pedro, he's content to be a dreamer. . .

So was born Pedroheze, which Rodney said was particularly good for sticking rope to mahogany.

Rodney eventually went off to live in Exeter with the intention of being an architect, I believe. I am sure that if we met again he would recall not only these little ditties, but the entire words we put to the Sousa march *Stars and Stripes for Ever*, from

> Samuel Mumford sitting in the middle of a field of
> roasted peanut popcorns
>
> Samuel Mumford sitting in the middle of a field of new-
> mown hay . . .

all the way through to

> And now I must say Adieu!
> Adieu, Adieu, a duty-free tobacco!

A friend of a very different type was Audley Edward (Ted) Southcott. He was held in awe in the sixth form because he had been out to work before returning to school – perhaps for only a few months – and so we thought him mature and worldly-wise. He came from a peculiar bohemian family in Newport; at least they seemed bohemian to me because, unlike the strict regimen at Whitecroft Farmhouse, they would have meals when they felt like it, even in the middle of the night. Or they would throw a party, just because it was Thursday. Armagh regarded them with heavy suspicion, and was not happy with my friendship, feeling ill at ease when Audley visited us at Whitecroft.

Ted Southcott attracted me because his interests were my interests – literature, politics, sex – and his real or supposed maturity meant that he was further along the road to grappling confidently with them. But what drew us together most was our mutual empathy. We could pick up half-expressed thoughts instantly: whole sentences were rarely necessary because our minds were going along similar tracks. Add to this the fact that we were both intoxicated with our new discovery of the

131

world of ideas, and we have a recipe for putting all art, politics and sex to rights. Once when he visited me at Whitecroft we both walked all the way back to his home in Newport, and, as the conversation was so heady, when we got there we turned round and walked back to Whitecroft again. Luckily this was at dead of night, because he tended to shout his comments on philistinism, communism, and free love in public places.

Audley Southcott later became a designer for television, but his name disappeared from the credits after a show in which he had bishops capering about with candles. Although nothing remarkable by today's standards, this was thought a bit too much for the taste of the time. Southcott could be regarded as the first of my adult friends, marking a significant stage in my growing up.

CHAPTER NINE

Growing up

There were only four students in my year of the sixth form. Apart from myself they were Audrey Caine, Ted Southcott whom we have met, and the beautiful Pamela Abrahams. Like many attractive girls Pamela gained maturity and poise because of the number of social contacts her good looks brought her: older people liked talking to her and doubtless some went out of their way to help her. I noticed that Greatwood, our headmaster, enjoyed innocently chatting her up in our French lessons in his study. Pamela went on to a place at Oxford.

The sixth form was very different from the rest of the school, and not only because of its small size. The changed atmosphere was epitomised by Taffy Davies, the geography teacher, when, to my great astonishment, he *suggested* rather than told us to do some exercise or read some book. The small numbers meant that classes were more like tutorials. Also, with so few teachers in contact with so few students it was possible to see what a seminal effect a good teacher has, although the full realisation of what I owe to these three or four staff came only after I had left school.

For the Higher School Certificate (the forerunner of 'A' levels) I took English, French and Geography as main subjects, and Latin at a subsidiary level. Lower down the school two decisions had been made about my academic programme. Firstly, it was considered that I had a chance of entering university (this at a time when entry was far more competitive) and that I would therefore need to think of a suitable package of subjects to study in the sixth form. Secondly, I needed maths if I were to take a science package, Latin for arts. I was hopeless at maths and I had never studied Latin. Luckily, I was otherwise an all rounder, so the rest of either package would cause no problem. The solution was to rush me through a one-year Latin crash course in the fifth form with the Eton cropped Miss Rabley. I still can recite the beginning of the sixth book of the Æneid:

Sic fatur lacrimans...

Miss May Mackenzie and Miss Ida Beck took us for English, but the former came and went on temporary appointments, and it was the latter who was principally responsible for our English studies in the sixth form. It was Miss Beck's inspiration which led to my taking English rather than one of my other subjects at university. I first thought that she had a slight speech impediment, because she seemed to pronounce words in a clumsy and deliberate way, giving almost equal weight to the accented and the unaccented syllables of a word. But there was nothing amiss: she came from Hull, and so had an accent which was strange to us. It is a southernism (and hence standard English) to swallow unaccented syllables (thus - cómftble). Miss Beck seemed to manage *two* accents in 'dífficúlty'.

In any event she opened up to us the world of modern

literature, in particular 'adult' authors of whom my mother would not approve – Aldous Huxley, Richard Aldington, D.H. Lawrence. At last she got me to read. Miss Beck had a good, if wayward, pupil in Audley Southcott, because he had done some reading and had firm ideas. He was obsessed at the time with Garcia Lorca. In the previous year Miss Beck had run a wider class to introduce literature to the whole of the fifth form, scientists and all. Two scientists – Gordon Philpot and Des Russell – resisted fiercely, thinking it all a waste of time, and resenting the loss of time which could have been spent in the laboratory.

The war continued and we still had air raids. At one period they occurred frequently in school time and the routine when we heard the siren was to leave everything and run down Medina Avenue to the air raid shelters on the edge of the town football ground at Church Litten, quite a distance. We were losing a lot of school time this way, so a new régime was instituted whereby we would rush to the shelters, and when we were all assembled the teacher would attract attention with a little cough, and attempting to control breathlessness, would resume teaching with "Now as I was saying . . ." and carry on, using large sheets of paper instead of a blackboard.

Some raids were of merely nuisance value, to set off the air raid warnings, send people scurrying to shelters, and so disrupt life. One such happened just as I was getting up at Whitecroft to go to school. Looking out of the window I saw three Messerschmidt 109 fighters screaming past at just rooftop height; indeed one had to bank to clear the hospital clock tower.

All buildings had to have a fire watching team on duty every night, to deal promptly with any incendiary bombs which might come raining down. The school teams were made up from staff and the sixth form, an arrangement which loosened the then somewhat formal relationship between teacher and taught, and probably aided the process of growing up. Now and again on a summer night we would take our beds out on to the roof where the only division between male and female was the chimney stack, which could be walked around in a few steps. There were suspicions of goings-on between Ted Southcott and the handsome young art teacher, Dorothy Hope.

Miss Mackenzie had fine breasts. I had noticed them in class when she stretched, raising her arms in her white cable-knit sweater. And she noticed that I noticed. This might have accounted for the little embarrassment I felt when I found myself fire-watching with her; the two of us alone in the staff room. Finding conversation difficult, I delved into the book cupboard and seized the first textbook that came to hand. Inevitably it was the *Merchant of Venice* which I had bumped into all the way up the school. I started declaiming from wherever the book fell open: it was where Bassanio hits the jackpot and discovers Portia's portrait in the casket

> ... What find I here?
> Fair Portia's counterfeit! What demi-god
> Hath come so near creation? Move these eyes?

Here I reached the foot of the page, and just before turning over remembered how the passage continued. Doubtless the good Miss Mackenzie did too. But I could not stop abruptly in mid-flow so I bravely forged on

> Or whether riding on these balls of mine,
> Seem they in motion?. . .

As soon as I could get away with it, I stopped. "That's enough of that!" I brightly said, and Miss Mackenzie did not demur.

Despite wartime restrictions some visits to the theatre were arranged by the school. Theatres were in most instances converted cinemas, because long before the general decline of the cinema in the face of television a young entrepreneur was flitting about the Island changing over many of our cinemas to theatres, not, it must be said, in response to popular demand. His name was Bernard Delfont. We were sick of billboards shouting "BERNARD DELFONT PRESENTS . . . It was to one of these theatres – the Commodore at Ryde - that a visit was arranged by Miss Rabley to see *The Mikado*. I did not go, not because of lack of money or parental permission, but because I did not know what it was all about: I had never heard of Gilbert and Sullivan and a Japanese musical play did not seem my cup of tea at all. Had I gone, my enjoyment of G and S would have started years sooner.

One event I did attend was a sixth form conference arranged by the Council for Education in World Citizenship at Queenswood School in Hertfordshire. To my astonishment I was called upon there to present a paper on religion in India, a subject on which I knew nothing, so my audience got regurgitated textbook. Two notable people were there. One was Hewlett Johnson, the Dean of Canterbury – the "Red Dean". A jolly man, red-faced, white-haired and black-gaitered. The other was Hilary Rubinstein, a lad of my own age who not only took part in the conference but seemed to have some part in organising it. I was to meet him again a year or so later in the Air Force in Torquay . Now he is a literary agent and the editor of *The Good Hotel Guide*.

A regular commitment on one night a week was the meeting of the Air Training Corps. It was held at the school, but there was a gap between the end of classes and the beginning of ATC activities in which I would go down to the town to get a meal. I regularly bestowed my custom on Cheek's Dairy in Pyle Street: the building is still there, facing St Thomas's Square, but it is now a Nearly New shop. This was presided over by a large lady, presumably Mrs Cheek: I assumed that it was her husband who was behind the serving hatch sweating over a hot stove. It was a workman's dining room rather than a dairy and indeed offered only one dish – egg, sausage and baked beans. This I would ask for, spelling out all the ingredients, and Mrs Cheek would go over to the hatch and bellow through it "Meal!". The ritual went on week after week, but eventually I could see no point in specifying "Egg, sausage and beans, please" if this was to be immediately translated into "Meal!". So one day I ventured to ask for "a meal please", which occasioned a look of utter puzzlement on the large lady's face. What sort of meal? she enquired, and when I spelled out "Egg, sausage and beans" again she was quite happy, going over to the hatch and singing out, "Meal!"

We have already said that the Commanding Officer of our flight of the ATC was Flight Lieutenant D.H. Greatwood, our headmaster and French teacher. He did not cut a particularly military figure in his fine serge uniform; he was short and plump so there were too many horizontal creases. Not all the cadets were his pupils during the day, but those – like me – who were could accept him as a different person in the evening. Except on one occasion. The usual Flight Sergeant who drilled the flight on parade was absent, so Greatwood cast about for the most senior cadet present. This was a long serving, aimiable, but idle lad called Colin Du Feu (another Channel Island name?) anglicised to De Few. Greatwood recognised no anglicisation, however. In the fruitiest dark brown accent of the devoted French scholar he commanded "Go and get me Cadet Du Feu . . ." and seeing our astonishment at his Gallic *tour de force* added ". . . or however he pronounces his name".

My memories of our activities at the ATC are hazy, but I imagine we must have studied the principles of navigation and had much practice in aircraft recognition. One skill we certainly acquired was the Morse Code. Like riding a bicycle, this is an accomplishment once learned, never forgotten, and even now I could rattle off a message for you if required. We were taught by Mr H.O. Lewis, whom we revered because he had written a slim pamphlet on the subject. But the highlights of my time in the ATC were the visits we made, both on and off the Island.

A very unofficial sort of visit was the weekly trip on a Sunday morning to Wootton Creek with the intention of going sailing. This was thought to be useful in teaching us navigation, but we suspected that the real reason for going was that whoever organised it liked sailing. Our intentions were never realised; we never set foot in a boat. The plan was that an instructor would come to meet us at Wootton and take us out in his boat, but not once did he arrive, so we had many wasted journeys. The defaulting mariner was one Vic Colleypriest, and the rumour was that on the Sunday mornings in question he was abed with a lady in Shanklin. So I composed, to the tune of *Jealousy*:

> Colleypriest! That sod of a Colleypriest!
> Our tryst was broken
> We could not go boat'n . . .
>
> 'Twas all over Vic Colleypriest
> (That sod of a Colleypriest!)
> 'Twas all over Vic Colleypriest . . .

We made several visits to what must have been our nearest military airfield, Lee-on-the-Solent, near Gosport, then readily identified by its tower, later taken down or bombed flat. This was a Fleet Air Arm, not an RAF station, so our guides were naval officers and the aircraft were not the usual land-based fighters and bombers. The most thrilling flight of my life was in an open cockpit Swordfish, wind screaming through the struts and wires between the two wings. The pilot put her into a spin. The effect of a spin is that the plane seems motionless but that the world gyrates crazily round and round. I remember being fascinated by gazing at a farmhouse directly below, in the centre of our spin – the calm eye of the storm, so to speak – it was slowly twisting round and round through 360° as though transfixed on the spindle of a turntable.

We were still following the Royal Navy rather than the Royal Air Force when we went to see Whale Island, the Navy gunnery school in Portsmouth Harbour. We could see at once that this was the home of Navy 'bull', with whitewashed stones bordering the paths, and doubtless whitewashed coal too. We were taken on a tour of inspection of all the guns ranged around the perimeter of the island. The Petty Officer conducting us made the distinction between guns which had a light over the breech to aid loading, and those which did not. In the latter case he said "You have to feel for the hole – like when you are out with a Wren", and then was immediately overcome with embarrassment as he realised that his listeners were aged sixteen or seventeen, were unfamiliar with the forces 'learning by filth' technique, and had never been out with a Wren in their lives.

We must have spent some days at a stretch at Lee on-the-Solent or Whale Island, because at one station we were subject to the extraordinary 'liberty boat' procedure which obtains at Navy shore stations. Such land-based establishments are treated as ships as far as possible; they use terms such as galley and wardroom, and the names sound like ships too – *HMS Dolphin, HMS Vernon* (Actually His/Her Majesty's *Station*). When you go off duty for the evening, you cannot simply walk out of the gate, you must wait for the next 'liberty boat', which might not leave for another hour. When the time arrives, you merely march out of the gate in a squad.

The ATC once went on a joint camp with the Sea Cadets. They had an aggressive little Chief Petty Officer who would bring his parade to attention with the cry of "Sea Cadets, Tcha!", his version of "'Shun!" Quite uncharacteristically I found the devilment to pinch his

141

jersey with his CPO insignia and dash about the camp shouting "Tcha! Tcha!" to all and sundry. I thought the end of the world would come in retribution, (my father told me to beware of short NCOs) but all was taken in good part.

It was at the same camp that I met a fellow cadet named Emmett. He came from another flight and was a member of a big family in Freshwater. I recall him with affection, perhaps because he flattered me. He seemed to be greatly taken by my vocabulary and the odd *bon mot* which came from me in conversation. His response to each instance was "Ah! Pretty good, mate! I'll put that down in my little book!" (*Aaah! Perdy good mate! Oil put that down in moi lill book!*). It may be supposed that the countryman's prefatory "Ah!" is a way of delaying speech so that he has a bit more time to marshal his thoughts, but I have heard people greet one another with no more than a single "Aah!"

During all this time I was studying for my Higher School Certificate. I took the exams in the summer of 1944, just about the time of D Day and the fighting to push the Germans out of northern France. Naturally conscription was in force, and I had to obtain deferment of my call-up until my examinations were over. Even then, I joined the Royal Air Force in a special way, via a University Air Squadron. The object of this scheme was to encompass the first (ground) stages of aircrew training at a university so that other, more traditional, academic subjects could be studied concurrently. This was thought suitable for potential officers. It was apparently deemed important that we should be gentlemen by the time we were shot down over Essen . . .

Selection for a University Air Squadron place was at the Recruitment Office in Portsmouth. Several of us were in an outer room waiting to be interviewed by the Recruitment Officer himself and were getting a pep talk from a more junior colleague, apparently of First World War vintage. He repeatedly urged us "Do stress to the officer how keen you are to get at the Hun!" This kind of phraseology was not in my vocabulary, and I cannot remember if I found myself able to mouth the words when the time came. But I was accepted.

I was offered a fair list of universities from which to choose (although not all took part in the scheme, and there were fewer in total before the great expansion of the 1960s). Oxford and Cambridge were among them, but I blew my chances in that direction through sheer naïveté. I said I would like to go to either, and my lack of differentiation showed that I had no knowledge of or connections with the one or the other, so I could give no convincing reason for my choice. Being then promptly told that they were full, I chose Durham solely on the grounds that it was the furthest from home, as far as I knew. (I was wrong – St Andrews was also on the list.) I knew no more about Durham than I did about Oxbridge, but I was to find out within a couple of months. I am now proud to regard myself as an honorary Geordie.

CHAPTER TEN

Taking flight

The streets of Durham are steep
And paved with granite setts

This is not part of a poem, but a prose sentence from the information sent to me on the Island before I first set out for Durham. Its rhythm made it echo in my mind in time to my steps as I trudged up Silver Street from Framwellgate Bridge to Palace Green.

Palace Green was the heart of the university; a large square lawn between castle and cathedral, flanked by lecture rooms, the library, and the students' union. Unlike more modern civic universities, Durham had a collegiate system, but since all teaching was centralised, colleges were little more than halls of residence and foci for sporting loyalties. My college was housed in the castle, and was therefore always called Castle (*Cassel* – with a flat but short Northern 'a'), and never University College, its proper name. So I was, indeed I still am, a Castleman.

The only other general college for men in Durham was Hatfield College (named after a Bishop, not the town). During the war we had the indignity of Hatfield sharing our dining room in the Great Hall of the castle.

By a sharp blow on a bent spoon one could project a pea in a high trajectory to land, if one scored a bulls-eye, in the water glass of the Hatfield Senior Man. There were other war-time arrangements. The two theological colleges, St John's and St Chad's, were reduced in size and accommodated together: I overheard someone in the Union say "Actually I *am* Chad's College". Even more odd was the situation of the teacher training colleges. The College of the Venerable Bede (Bede for short) had vacated its premises to accommodate Whitelands College which had been evacuated from London. The cheer-leaders' cry was bizarre, "B! E! D! E! Whitelands!"

Part of our time was spent in RAF studies. My weakness in mathematics made my navigation shaky, but I had a physical reason for worrying about my Morse Code. Just before going to Durham I had been engaged in a friendly battle with Eric Prangnell at Whitecroft, lobbing clods of dirt at one another. One containing a stone hit me in the eye, causing no permanent damage, but for a time the tendency to water when under strain. So I had difficulty in picking up Aldis lamp signals at maximum speed. I confided my problem to the gruff and kindly Scots instructor, Pilot Officer Hay. Whether he fiddled it or not I don't know, but the first words he said after the crucial official test was "You're through, New". He was not as agreeable, however, when he had to investigate who had been, at dead of night, sending indecent Aldis signals from the castle keep to the roof of the science laboratories.

Another officer instructed us in gunnery: I think his name was Roberts. This nice shy man had the task of teaching us how to strip the Browning machine gun. In order that we might not only take it to pieces but successfully put it together again, we needed to know what all the constituent bits were. So there was a 'naming of parts' almost as ludicrous as that in the poem of that title. There was a little component called a sear, which was actuated by a spring. This spring was kept in place by a retainer, but experience had shown that this was not enough, because the retainer was retained by a keeper. I can no longer remember what a sear spring retainer keeper looks like, but its name lives on in my memory.

These instructors seemed a little old for such junior commissioned rank – Pilot Officer or Flying Officer. My guess is that they had seen much aircrew service as NCOs, and as a relief or because of wounds had been put on instructor duties with a commission. Perhaps officer teachers were thought essential for officer cadets. In any event we liked them, and their obvious war experience earned our respect. Our non-commissioned officers were appointed from among ourselves, after a series of leadership tests. The most senior – our Flight Sergeant – was Howard Phelps, later to become Director of Operations of British Airways and then a director of P & O. He is a big man. While bearing in mind my father's fear of short NCOs, I believe that tall men start with a built-in advantage in the leadership stakes. I write as a shortarse.

More memorable were our academic studies, if only because our teachers were so prone to parody that I was furnished with a party piece for years to come. Dr (later Sir) James Duff took us for American History. He was the Warden of the Durham Colleges, a sort of Vice-Chancellor for the Durham (as distinct from the

Newcastle) Division of the university. He sniffed twice in every sentence and made frequent reference to Stonewall Jackson, and his favourite little textbook, apparently by Nevins, Sniff, and Commager. Canon Richardson had a different problem – adenoids. All I remember of his philosophy lectures is his cocking his head in the air and adenoidally enquiring "How do we know that we know?". At that point I decided that epistemology was too mind-boggling to bother with.

Professor "Lefty" Hood (Politics) suffered from extreme myopia. So much so that he held his notes so close that they brushed his face, and one could see when he was about to turn over because his nose appeared at the bottom. The spectacle he presented to us was so absorbing that little attention was paid to what he was saying. I gathered that the war was all the fault of the Magyars and the Kuomintang: at least these were sonorous words which reverberated in my mind and which were raw material for my imitations, together with his harsh croak and the paper obscuring the face.

Edward Hughes, the Professor of History, was just eccentric. He had the habit of repeating his phrases over and over, presumably in a form of dictation so that one could write down his exact words. "I was dealing (like all good Mancunians he sounded his 'g's), I was dealing last time, At the end of my last lecture I was dealing with . . ." and so on. This was not the limit of his oddity. While all this repetition was going on he was flailing his arms about for emphasis. On one occasion I sat in the front row of the class, directly underneath him. Soon I found myself enveloped in the black silk of his gown, quite unable to see my notes and so take down his words if I

147

wanted to. Not only that. He was resting *his* notes on my head.

The other significant memory of this six months in Durham is being persuaded by a fellow student to go with him to the Spiritualist church. I cannot explain spiritualism, but I am convinced that it is not a hoax. For one thing, the practitioners I saw were not sophisticated enough to keep up an elaborate pretence. Indeed on the night I went, the medium had a strange and downmarket mode of speech. He would see a "presence" with one of the congregation, "I see a little blue light on your shoulder – not you dear, the lady behind the column. I see a gentleman in spirit clothing with a grey mouthtache [sic] and beard, about seventy years of age when he passed the Change Called Death." All his messages that evening ended in the same way, "He (or she) just puts his hand on your shoulder and says 'Alls wills bees well'". (Why is the 'other side' always bland and comforting?) We would have had possibly a less idiosyncratic performance the following week because we were promised as a visiting medium Mr Hook from Crook. The 'oo' in both was long, as in 'pool', not short, as in 'book'.

The other reason why I take spiritualism seriously is personal. The medium saw a blue light on *my* shoulder. He said that the person on the other side wishing to contact me was a boy of my own age who had died in an accident. I immediately thought of "Nugget" Constable, who had been killed by a horse (p29). I was then told that the boy appeared in a choirboy's cassock and surplice: this made me dismiss Nugget from my mind because I knew that he belonged to a Nonconformist church which did

148

not use vestments. So we were at an impasse. The medium was puzzled that I could not identify this person who, he said, was so close to me. He asked me to make enquiries when I was next on the Island, and when I did I found that Nugget's church *did* use surplices, a fact quite unknown to me. This seems to dispose of the "reading my subconscious mind" explanation of spiritualism. What the explanation is I do not know, but I would rather do without one than rationalise the unknowable, the bane of organised religions.

The same fellow cadet who introduced me to spiritualism went out with me one night to a pub where we got into conversation with a Royal Canadian Air Force warrant officer. In common with others in the forces, he affected an exaggerated and individual form of speech, perhaps on the principle that one must shout to be heard above the crowd. So instead of expressing mild incredulity with 'Oh yes?' or 'Is that so?' or even "I don't belive it!' he would thunder out, every time, "Don't give me the horseshit!" Of course, so much vehemence devalued the currency, as did his frequent oaths on his "Royal Canadian Ass".

After all this I joined the Air Force proper in Torquay as 3036338 AC2 New, P G, ACH-U/T PNB. All this meant that I was an aircraftman, second class, that my trade was aircrafthand (a catch-all to enable me to be used on any duties) and I was under training as a pilot, navigator, or bomb aimer. 1945 was a glorious spring and we marched around in shirt-sleeve order feeling like young gods, because we were told constantly that we were the élite, *la crème de la crème*, potential aircrew officers distinguished by a white flash in our forage caps.

149

Bliss was it in that dawn to be alive
But to be young was very heaven

Our squadron was made up of the cadets from Oxford as well as Durham and was based at the Endsleigh Hotel. The Cambridge lot were up the hill at the Devonshire.

We were fortunate in the NCOs assigned to be in charge of our squads. They were drill instructors, not thought the brightest personnel in the RAF, and it might be expected that they would have had much sarcastic fun at the expense of a bunch of academic recruits. Not so. Corporal Hollingsworth said not a word out of place, was firm, fair, kindly and caring. When we eventually left Torquay, he shook us each by the hand and had a personal word as we boarded the train. To me he said, "Try to keep your feet on the ground, New", a reference to my strange gait when marching, a quarter of a step out of phase with the rest of the squad, so that my head bobbed up when theirs bobbed down.

One of my squad was Hilary Rubinstein whom I had met a year or so earlier at the sixth form conference at Queenswood School. As we marched around Torquay in the sun, I became aware of highly intellectual conversation taking place in the rank behind me. It was Hilary, deep into literary criticism with his friend. The friend was so focussed on the world of ideas that he was placed on a charge for allowing his shoes to be worn down, well beyond the leather, to the wooden core of the heels. He just hadn't noticed. I still do not know who this friend was. He was freckled and had wavy brown hair and striking blue eyes: Frederic Raphael would fit the

150

description but is five years too young. Godfrey Smith, now of the *Sunday Times*, was also in the squad, but I did not know him at the time.

I recall remarkably few people from that squad at Torquay. One is memorable only because his name – Melhuish – caused a little difficulty to the Good Corporal Hollingsworth at roll-call. He was not sure whether or not to pronounce as spelt, and sometimes nervously rushed out with "Mellish!" Standing on parade in the hot sun I abstractedly observed aloud, "Mr Melhuish thinks the weather is hellhuish . . ." Not very funny, and I was surprised at hearing a titter ripple through the ranks behind me.

I had met 3024242 Eric Rhodes at Durham and we were together for a time in the RAF afterwards. He was a modest little Scotsman who had much sport in encouraging me to entertain the barrack room with my wilder eccentricities. (Imitation of my professors was the milder part.) I have a sharp picture in my mind of Eric fainting when he was sitting next to me in the mess-hall: his head slid down my chest until it dunked itself comprehensively in my soup.

Whilst we were at Torquay the war in Europe came to an end. Part of the VE Day celebrations was a parade of the armed services before the Mayor of Torquay and the local populace. So we, not yet nineteen years old and with some three weeks' service to our credit, took the plaudits of the good folk of Torquay for winning the war for them. The event itself was a classic military cock-up. The music got out of phase with the marching, so we saluted the dais to the tune of "Anchors Aweigh", and the army, following us, did so to the strains of the RAF March Past. Victory or not, the morning before the parade was business as usual. We were running down a hill and bayoneting sacks, to the accompaniment of fearsome screams.

It is difficult to see the relevance of bayoneting sacks to training for aircrew, but the time came when we were really going to learn to fly. The first stage was Grading School which was to determine if we had the aptitude to be pilots, or if we would be navigators or bomb aimers instead. I have no doubt that if our training had been completed I would have ended up prone on my tum in the belly of a bomber pressing the button to let the bombs go. My mathematics would have made me an unreliable navigator – I would have steered a 'reciprocal' course (ie exactly opposite to my intended direction) and bombed the hell out of Reykjavik instead of Berlin. I was barely the minimum height for a pilot and had difficulty in reaching the rudder bar with my feet. After the twelve hours' flying instruction at Grading School, I was not one of those allowed to fly solo. As a point of honour I had to ask to do so, but the refusal of my request probably ensured my survival to write this account.

Grading School was at Brough, on the bank of the Humber west of Hull. We shared the airfield with the Blackburn aircraft factory, and we had to clear the runways of our little Tiger Moths when Blackburns wanted to try out their new fighter for the Fleet Air Arm (Firebrand?). The Tiger Moth was a lovely little old-fashioned biplane with a touch of the amateur about it: the petrol gauge was a bent nail arrangement up on the top wing, and no-one expected it to work. The 'plane was easy for beginners to fly, but, so they said, it was difficult to fly really well.

Our flying instructors, with many hours of flying more sophisticated aircraft to their credit, took liberties with the Tiger Moth – but only when flying solo. They would roar across the airfield at rooftop height and bump their wheels on the roof of the hut in which we were assembled, fully kitted up, waiting for our turn to fly. Or instead they would momentarily cut the motor, and from a similar height would yell out to their colleagues on the ground, "Get in the air!".

By contrast, our efforts were much more tentative. Looking out over the airfield it was not uncommon to see the indignity of a couple of Tiger Moths up-ended, tails in air. Obviously a rough landing, the trickiest part of flying. For myself, I found flying 'straight and level' quite hard enough. My instructor was, unfortunately, Flight Lieutenant Savage, who could not have been more aptly named. Finding that I was incapable of executing the manoeuvre he had planned, he asked me to fly straight and level following a railway line below. Easier said than done. The body of the plane conceals what is directly below, and I found that the railway line was poking out beneath the fuselage at a steep angle, first on one side, then on the other. Savage was furious, and I was blasted through my headphones. When he was annoyed F/Lt Savage had the nasty habit of "stirring the pudding". He would roll the joystick round and round, making the plane pitch, bank, yaw, and nearly stall, then he would say to his whey-faced pupil, "Now get out of that!"

Our main mode of training was "circuits and bumps". The drill was to take off into the wind (usually westward), turn left across the Humber, climb to 1,000 feet, turn left again on the downwind leg along the Lincolnshire coast, then crosswind again, cut the motor and make a gliding turn into the wind to land. Shortly before landing one should ease the joystick back to make the aircraft stall about six inches above the ground. To gauge when this was necessary, we were told to look over the side of the fuselage and wait for the point at which we could distinguish individual blades of grass. (I wonder if they tell the pilots of jumbo jets to do this?)

One of my attempts at circuits and bumps was a little different. I roared up to 1,000 feet quite satisfactorily, but it was on the descent where I went wrong. I got to the point of looking over the side to see the individual blades of grass, and was horrified to see nothing of the sort, but angry little waves instead. I had cut the motor one leg too soon, and was gliding in to alight, Christ-like, on the Humber. In the event of error the correct procedure is to apply full throttle to climb up to 1,000 feet and go round again. Not me. I gave just enough gas to putter in at an altitude of about twenty feet, and flopped thankfully to earth just inside the boundary hedge. I am not sure if it was on that or another occasion when I narrowly missed landing on top of the specially bulled-up Tiger Moth reserved for the Commanding Officer. As I said, it is difficult to see what is directly below.

After Grading School it was all anti-climax. The next stage should have been the main part of our aircrew training, possibly in Canada or Rhodesia under the Empire Air Training Scheme, but the war was coming to an end, so we did a lot of waiting while decisions were made. First we waited in tents and huts in Heaton Park in Manchester. The road outside was illuminated by prison-like yellow sodium lights, but even more like a prison, the walls were smeared with grease, and our trousers were inspected every day for indications that we had climbed out the night before.

The authorities did not know what to do with us and there was an air of demoralisation. We were idle for much of the time: passing one tent I overheard one gambling Scot say to another, "That'll be twenty seven pound ten you're owing me now Jock". We would spend as long as we liked at the local municipal swimming pool, with the object of upgrading our ability to the level required of aircrew. During the test, the corporal in charge nipped out for a smoke, so I put my feet down and trudged along. No doubt I *could* swim 100 yards if my plane ditched and my life depended on it . . .

One day an officer told us that a corporal would march us to a Nissen hut and give us a lecture on signals. When we were seated in the hut and the officer had gone, the little cockney corporal rubbed his hands and said, "Nah boys, we don't want to talk about signals do we? Lets have a discussion group! What subject shall we take? Sex?" And away we went. But Heaton Park was not a complete loss. I had plenty of time to go into Manchester and join the great round Central Library (the British Museum of the North). I got to know Milton there.

Eventually a decision (very reasonable from the RAF's viewpoint) was made that we would continue with flying training only if we undertook to remain in the service for some years after the date at which we would otherwise be released. Some gave the undertaking but thought they could evade their part of the bargain. Those like me who declined the offer would be "misemployed", that is, given a miscellany of unskilled ground duties, until we were "remustered" or given a permanent ground trade, presumably with the requisite training.

One of my misemployments was at RAF Eastchurch, on the Isle of Sheppey, later an open prison. My moment of heady power was when I was temporarily in charge of the Vegetable Room, but – alas! – my initiative was my downfall. Shutting up for the night I noticed a tap dribbling into a vast sink containing some tons of peeled potatoes. So I turned it off. The next morning the spuds had taken on a decidedly pink colour and they smelled of gin.

Our most peculiar task was helping with the harvest on a farming detachment at Lower Whitley on the Cheshire/Lancashire border, where I did very little work because I developed blisters, just like I do at tennis. There were only six of us, in the charge of a corporal who had the most delicious delusions of grandeur. He insisted on our obtaining the proper RAF pass if we wanted a weekend off, and he would sign it as follows:

> Henry Blenkinsopp (or whatever his name was), Corporal.
> Officer Commanding, RAF Station Lower Whitley, Nr
> Warrington.

My longest misemployment was at Cranwell in Lincolnshire, the home of RAF bull. Ironically this was where my colleagues who had opted to stay on were continuing their flying training, but I was a humble equipment assistant. I had some advantages over them: permanent staff is not subject to the strict discipline which is applied to trainees. And I had the perks of my adopted trade. Some of the equipment staff had been tailors in civilian life, and they would fuss about one, making the inherently baggy battledress fit as snugly as possible. We also had the dodge (later rumbled) of handing in our equipment and getting in its place a 'deficiency chit', which should be issued only when the stores run out of stock of an item. But a piece of paper is much more convenient to carry than a steel helmet!

One evening I was on night duty with a WAAF who was making a watch strap for herself out of a length of thin Pilot Officer's stripe. Picking up a piece I tucked it around my shoulder strap just for fun and forgot it. Later I went to the cook-house to collect our supper, and I could not understand why the cook was hopping about so attentively. Impersonating an officer is a grave offence, but the only crime for which I was caught was "failing to stand to attention when the ensign was being lowered at 20.00 hours, contrary to Section 40 of the Air Force Act". (I was seen to scuttle between two huts.) Section 40 is the catch-all "conduct prejudicial to good order and military discipline" and like most of the Air Force Act, is a scarcely adapted copy of the Army Manual. So one is required to deport oneself in an "airmanlike" manner, the equivalent of "soldierly". Should one flap the arms about, like wings?

I found that an easy way to gain popularity in the barrack hut was to trot out my party pieces. In this I would be egged on by Eric Rhodes or others. As well as the imitations of my professors at Durham I had developed childish actions to fit the names of the railway stations from Manchester Victoria, through Heaton Park, to Bury. Thus to Crumpsall I would crash my feet down to the ground, Besses o' th' Barn would call for a somersault on to my bed, and at the final shout of "Bury! I would dive head first into the bedclothes. Great roars of laughter – *at* me, not *with* me. One who did not laugh was a serious Scot named Miller, older than most of us, and a poet. Why he chose me I do not know – I think there was no improper motive – but he would ask me to come and sit on his bed to hear his "verrse". After playing to the gallery I was ashamed and embarrassed when someone took me seriously. But I must accept that facetiousness is an ineradicable part of my nature.

CHAPTER ELEVEN

Castleman

It was easy to go back to Durham after the war. My previous essays were referred to and judged to be of a satisfactory level. The influence of the good Miss Beck at school was still powerful enough to make it obvious that I would choose Honours English.

The problem was not in the choice of the main subject but the subsidiary. Of my other sixth form subjects, I could not contemplate French because I was much too nervous of speaking a modern foreign language, and as I was not strong enough in Latin only Geography was left. I was keen to do this but it was not possible because it counted as a science and therefore would not timetable with the arts and humanities. So *faute de mieux* I took History, a subject I actively dislike, but I had at least studied it up to fifth form level at school.

The first year of subsidiary History was encouraging. We were lectured on English social history of the nineteenth century by Professor Edward Hughes (he of the repetitions whom we have met before – p147). Perhaps this topic suited me, but in any event I did so well that Hughes thought I must be taking Honours Politics or something nearer History than English. Also I was beginning to develop academic ploys in essays and exam papers: I saw the value of throwing in a few sharp details, however irrelevant, to give the impression of a comprehensive mastery of fact. I promised myself that I would somehow get in the trivial information that Peel obtained the first Double First on record at Oxford. I did, and possibly this contributed to my success.

The second year was very different. This time it was European history of the nineteenth century taken by a gent sporting the name of Emile Henry Ugo de Groot. I would have found this subject boring anyway but de Groot became bogged down on two topics, presumably his own research interests. So we ground on for week after week on the Congress of Vienna, clause after tedious clause. When we had finished that we soon got locked into the minutiae of the negotiations preceding the Crimean War. I found the repeated journeys of Sir Stratford de Redcliffe not only wearisome but not worth committing to memory, because nothing seemed to come of them. I don't think we ever reached 1914, which is where the course should have ended.

Emile de Groot is firmly fixed in my mind for two different reasons. Firstly, for his unusual (albeit correctly Spanish) pronunciation of Trafalgár, with the accent on the last syllable. Doubtless he would also say Himálayas and Caríbbean (both with the accent on the second syllable). Secondly, because he failed me in History, twice. Once at the end of the second year, and once at the resit in September. To gain my degree I would then have to go down for a year and take History again in the following June. Luckily I was saved by a regulation, applicable to ex-servicemen, which allowed for an unclassed honours

160

degree with fewer papers being taken.

So I dropped one or two papers and carried on to my third year. By this time I had decided that I was going to be a librarian, and in that profession graduates were then in a minority, so the lack of a classed degree would seem to be no handicap. (Indeed I found later that it was wise to conceal one's degree when applying for jobs at some public libraries.) It never occurred to me to question de Groot's judgment, or to ask why the assessment of me differed so widely between the first and second year. Many years later I was teaching students who were of the generation which did question authority. This may be a healthy development but there can be unhappiness and uncertainty in challenging the accepted standards, and in refusing to accept the reality of failure.

At the end of my first year my results in English language were better than those in literature, so I was persuaded to become one of a new group specialising in Old and Middle English. The lecturer to lead us through the byways of *Beowulf* and *Sir Gawayne and the Grene Knight* was the delightful Bertram Colgrave. He was a totally unpretentious little man who would break off his commentary on some Anglo-Saxon poem when he saw the Bishop go past the lecture room window, "Oh that naughty man the Bishop! He still has my wheelbarrow – I gave him a load of manure on Saturday..." He did get himself somewhat distracted from his theme, and sometimes he made slips. When these were pointed out he would admit "You are quite right, Mr New, and I am quite wrong." I thought he looked grossly overworked, and I resolved that I would never allow myself to follow suit, but that is exactly what I did throughout my career.

161

Bertie never became fed up when I foisted Isle of Wight dialect on him; in fact he gratefully made marginal notes in his text. For example, we discovered that Sir Gawayne got harled (tangled) in the hedge, just like an Isle of Wighter. Bertie certainly had all the humility of the true scholar, but he did not put forward his claims in the conventional academic way – by publications. As far as I know his only book was *Two lives of St Cuthbert*, which left me facetiously puzzling, why two and not nine?

Our course demonstrated the way in which a curriculum is shaped by the specialisms of the academic staff. Because of Bertie's interest in the subject we had a paper on Germanic and Old English Antiquities – only somewhat distantly connected with English language and literature. In pursuit of this study we would be bundled into Bertie's large, ancient and sit-up-and-beg car (a Lanchester?) to see some of the nearby antiquities such as the site of Bede's monastery at Monkwearmouth or the 'megolithic quoining' at Escomb church. Bertie also infected us with his enthusiasm for the discovery of the Sutton Hoo ship burial – a fairly recent event.

The Professor of English was Claud Colleer Abbott. His main claim to fame was his discovery of Boswell papers at Fettercairn House in 1930. He had also done work on early medieval French lyrics and Gerard Manley Hopkins. It was said that the inner sanctum of his study (to which I was never invited) was adorned with pictures of nude boys. His task was to lead us through English poetry, but he did not seem too willing to do this, because his manner was always unpleasant. Clearly bored, he would flick through the copious pages of the *Faerie Queene*, saying "Not much here, I think . . . you must read it though!" From time to time he would irritably burst out with, "Writing, writing, writing! Why don't you put your pens down and listen to what I have to say?"

Thundered comments on the poems Claud was considering stick in my mind: ". . . a fresh May-morning atmosphere" and "the bitter tang of a Dunne or a Donne or however you pronounce his name . . ." His audience was granted, as a bonus to his booming words, a fair spattering of spittle. A further diversion was his odd pronunciation of 'room', 'bloom' etc, the long 'oo' sound being replaced by the short 'oo' as in 'cook':

> Nuns fret not in their convent's narrow room
> *What are you sniggering at, New?*

An example of the pernicketiness of the scholar and an insight into the professor's psychological make-up was provided by his observation: "In a sense – and only in a sense – it might possibly be said that Spenser was *sensuous* but not *sensual*. I don't want you to use that word." He further disconcerted us when we were reading out our long vacation essay to the class by interjecting "I don't agree with you, but go on!", thus pricking any pretentious bubbles of confidence we might have had. Pete Marsden had a stammer and so the plump Harold Morley read his essay for him. Claud took great pleasure in introducing Morley as Marsden's ghost, ". . . a very substantial ghost . . ."

It is amazing that I retain any affection for English

poetry after such an eccentric and bad tempered introduction. By contrast our exploration of English drama was superbly conducted. Clifford Leech was the perfect university lecturer, developing our insight by indicating depths we did not know were there. Indeed he seemed expert in finding explanations from the seamy side of life, sending off his students happily following up his 'incest theme'. Leech somehow looked the God-defying Renaissance man - unbelieving, dark and greasy of complexion, portly, and with faint egg stains on his shiny brown suit. But he, too, had the scholar's humility. In a tutorial with him I made an off-the-top-of-my-head attempt to explain a sub-plot in *Gorboduc* or some other pre-Shakesperian play. Leech took it seriously and tried it out, without mentioning my name, on his next tutorial student, Garry Philipson. Philipson, who roomed with me and squashed the idea flat, or so he told me later.

Clifford Leech also had the academic's concern for truth and for precision in the use of words. He gently chided me for using 'tragedy' in the common loose sense, when it should refer only to a dramatic form, and he would not accept "a Donne, a Marlowe, a Shakespeare" which a number of us had caught from the professor. At about this time I thought that I might become a journalist, and I had the misapprehension that journalists wrote in a flowery style. I had to write an essay on Allegory, with reference to poetry, prose and drama. I do not recall if it was Leech or Abbott who made the marginal comment, in a neat, tiny, scholarly hand, "Are you trying to *sell* the *Faerie Queene*?" Leech later became professor, and then moved on to Canada.

The other member of the English lecturing team was

John Parr Curgenven. It was said that Leech found him wandering about in Turkey, and brought him back to Durham. It might have been true, because he was totally ill-equipped for the severe winters of northern England. Dull and nervous, he droned on about the eighteenth century wearing two overcoats and with his nose blue and sporting a perpetual dewdrop. Not surprisingly he fell ill and was confined to the sick bay with shingles. Heartlessly, I led a group of undergraduates in serenading him with an adaptation of *John Brown's body*. You will remember that at each repetition the last word of the line is dropped. Just as well, because my version went:

John Parr Curgenven's got the shingles on his bum

The number of English lecturers was small because the student body was small. The Durham Division of the university was only about nine hundred students strong, whereas there were some four thousand in the Newcastle Division (later to become Newcastle University). This meant that we knew everyone in our own college and the most notable people in others. There was a strong sense of community, and although the university contrasted sharply with he workaday market town outside the Palace Green area, there was little conflict between 'town' and 'gown'. I recall with great pleasure a conversation I had at a bus stop with a young miner, who had just come up from his shift complete with helmet, headlamp, and grimy face. The pleasure is not in what we said, but in the fact that we were able to converse with no trace of awkwardness. There was no servility on his part, and, I believe, no condescension on mine.

In my time there was just the beginning of expansion of the university, possibly influenced by the increased demand caused by the backlog of ex-service students. In nineteen forty-seven Princess (now Queen) Elizabeth came to lay the foundation stone of a new building for St Mary's College on a bleak hill overlooking the science laboratories. While the ceremony was going on there was a rather embarrassed silence, until someone patriotically called for three cheers for the princess. The ice having been broken, another called out "Whack-oh November twentieth then!" which was the date of her forthcoming wedding.

Apart from an occasional visit to The Three Tuns or some other pub (each college tended to have its own favoured hostelry) I did not go out into the town very often. Sometimes I would visit the Essoldo cinema up the hill near the station, and here I found double seats in the back row, a facility which Bernard Delfont had never offered on the Isle of Wight. We had to be back in Castle before the gates were closed for the night by the somewhat crabby keeper of the porter's lodge, Mrs Shaw.

Mrs Shaw had two contrasting daughters, Jesse and Cicely. Jesse was dark and gipsy-like: our fantasy was that she was wild and passionate. She had a small son, Geoffrey. Cicely was fair, curly-headed, and virginal. She served in the buttery and took a lot of chaff from the undergraduates who did their best to shock and embarrass her. In return she would supply that part of our food ration which we took to our rooms, clutched in the folds of our gowns, so that we could make our own refreshments at teatime or late at night. Not only food was rationed. A special irony was that we were sitting on top of one of the richest coalfields in the country, yet all we had to burn in the open fires in our rooms were a few inadequate buckets of 'nutty slack'. There were few nuts in it but an inordinate quantity of incombustible powdery slack. And those who remember will agree that the winter of 1947 was particularly severe.

Rather than go out, we found most of our extra-curricular activities within the university. I was for a time secretary of the college literary and debating society, and I had the dangerous task of inviting the testy Professor Abbott to speak to the motion that "a man's life... can be lived like a thing of magic still if he will be only obstinate, crafty, and lonely" (J C Powys). It was a bit close to home, and Professor Abbott declined. Much the best debate I heard at Durham was on the motion that "Marks and Spencer have done more for the welfare of humanity than either Marx or Spenser." Clifford Leech spoke in defence of Marx. He spoke well, if perhaps a little generally, we thought, but when he was at least a third of the way into his speech he paused and said, "I am sure that all my audience realises that the Marx I am referring to is Groucho Marx . . ."

A popular event attended by many undergraduates of all disciplines was the series of talks given by the new Professor of Music, Arthur Hutchings. He was a great humourist: indeed his inaugural lecture was entitled Music and Humour. It was attended by the other professors and the canons of the cathedral who were discomfited by Hutchings's irreverent jabs at the church. He also exhibited two public speaking ploys which I envied, though I lacked the dexterity to copy both in my later lecturing career. As he finished a page of notes he screwed it up into a neat ball and lobbed it to land in his upturned mortar board on the grand piano, building up into a steep pyramid. I could never do that. But I occasionally copied his other party piece, his pause in the middle of a lecture, the puzzled frown at the notes, and the remark, "I must have been drunk when I wrote this!" (Later note: months after writing this I was delighted to have confirmation of the mortar board story in Hutchings's obituary (*Times* 17 November 1989.)

Arthur Hutchings had written a book on Delius. The reviewer had written of it, "Professor Hutchings mars his work by referring throughout to the composer as Fred." That sums him up. There was no doubt that he was a genuine musician, but he preferred eccentricity to conventional patterns of behaviour. He even walked in a peculiar way, and I treasure in my memory the vignette of him striding across Palace Green, with little Geoffrey, Jesse Shaw's son, imitating his gait a few paces behind.

I did attend one or two services in the cathedral and heard Professor Michael Ramsey preach. Durham, being strong in theology, had two professors of divinity, and Ramsey was the Van Mildert, as distinct from the Lightfoot professor. He was a few years later persuaded to take up a chair at Cambridge, but Durham soon brought up its biggest guns to get him back – he was made bishop and after that, the archbishoprics of York and Canterbury. He was an impressive and mannered speaker, his arm rising slowly until the swift descent at the climax. But a little religion goes a long way, and in general I found the proximity of the cathedral a nuisance, the bells waking me up when I wanted to snooze on a Sunday morning.

Part of the castle was open to the public. When I did get up on a Sunday morning I would be in the Junior Common Room reading the *News of the World* when there would be the sound of multiple shuffling feet outside. The visitors had reached the first stop in the guided tour of the castle – the Norman chapel, now restored, but then an open space of sweating flagstones with a sprinkling of litter. The shuffling would stop and the guide would begin her piece. "This is the oldest part of the castle (*cassel*) built in 1070, thirty years before the commencement of the building of the cathedral . . ." These stilted words never varied because they were learned by heart by the guides – our waitresses in the Great Hall. I wonder what happened if someone asked a question.

In my time, University College was in fact accommodated in *two* castles, because after the war we were also using Lumley Castle at Chester-le-Street for first year students. In charge was Colonel Leonard Slater, notable mainly for the fact that he retained his army rank in civilian life to the great annoyance of the ex-servicemen who made up a big proportion of the undergraduates. He had the usual 'At home' reception for which he sent out cards, "Colonel and Mrs Slater request the pleasure of the company of . . .". Our colleague Stan Morris responded, "Trooper Morris regrets."

If Slater was the "sub-master" at Lumley, the real Master of University College was Lt-Col A A Macfarlane-Grieve, MC MA, whose house was at the foot of the castle keep. He, too, had an 'At home'. At this event a group of us, including the above Stan Morris, found ourselves in

169

conversation with the Master's shy wife. The cliché 'locked in conversation' would be appropriate because we could not escape from the topic which engaged us. It was baths – short baths, long baths, hip baths, baths of every type. Sweaty and glassy-eyed, we struggled to free ourselves but could only keep the verbal merry-go-round spinning with enamelled baths, galvanised baths, officers' travelling baths . . .

It was said that the Master took a third class degree in mathematics. He lectured in military history, or would have done so if any students had offered themselves for it, and his sole publication was a history of Durham rowing. Despite his modest academic attainments he was an excellent master. He had shrewdly piloted the college through the war and the long period of shortages afterwards, and could resist the constant pressure from our Senior Man for better furniture, facilities and food with reason and courtesy. He was respected because he clearly had the interest of the college at heart: he was a Castleman himself. He could demonstrate a delicate touch. One morning we saw the following notice on the studded oak door of the Great Hall:

> The Master is grateful to gentlemen for their kind gifts of tin cans, orange peel and other objects thrown from the keep windows into his garden, but as he now has sufficient for his immediate requirements he requests that other means of disposal are found.

This ironic plea made for good master/student relationships, whatever its effectiveness. I do recall the odd item being lobbed out to the accompaniment of the cry, "The Master is grateful . . ." It was not only rubbish

170

which went out of the windows. The only lavatory for the keep was at its base, so that those living on the upper floors faced the prospect of a long freezing walk on icy stone flags if caught short on a winter night. So it was not unknown to open the window and let forth a high steaming trajectory faintly glinting in the first beginnings of dawn. It really was dawn when I had the urge. Up went the window – and luckily I stopped in time. Directly below the Master had paused in his morning jog around the keep and was squatting down to tie up his shoelace.

The Master, being a rowing enthusiast, would take on himself the duties of Honorary Coach to any passing boat he saw when strolling along the river banks. The crew of which I was cox was stopped several times and given gratuitous instruction in this way, yet I believe we won the Graduates' Cup through brute strength rather than practised technique. We rowed only in fours at Durham in my time although eights are used now. Our four was "Tink" Harper (bow), W.F. "Ben" Gunn (two), Garry Philipson (three), and Cameron Percy Crossley (stroke). Cam Crossley was a serious and humourless intending teacher: in one of his essays he had said that on balance he was against *capital* punishment for schoolchildren.

Unfamiliar Isle of Wight accents rebounded off the steep banks of the River Wear as I called out "In – Out!" (*In – Æut* in phonetic script) in the near-arctic dawn. I am not sure if our training in the early morning was because our scientist members had laboratory work in the afternoons, or whether it was no more than tradition. In any event it was mighty cold, and I, as cox, had the task of waking up the rest of the crew, an ironic duty for one so wedded to his bed. Frequently we encountered ice: on

171

one occasion we took out a two-man "tub" as an ice-breaker, with me in the bows with an old oar to thwack the floes ahead in order to crack open a channel. But alas! I was disconcerted to note a sheet of ice had penetrated the boat, so I issued a rapid recommendation to back-paddle. We just made the landing stage. I never got beyond college boating. I would have loved to obtain my 'Palat' (Palatinate Purple, the equivalent of an Oxbridge Blue) but there were enough university coxes ahead of me in seniority. The nearest I got was when the university boat was temporarily lodged in our boathouse. I ran my hand along the hull and remarked "Now I can say that I have stroked the university boat".

But the highlight of my rowing career at Durham was not winning the Graduates' Cup but overturning my boat under Elvet Bridge. Negotiating the bridge is tricky. The approach must be exact because there is only a foot or so of clearance each side, and almost immediately a turn has to be made to avoid running into the bank. On the day in question I was distracted by small boys on the parapet who were making rude V-signs at me. Forgetting the rule of "Always keep your eye in the boat" I responded in kind, and – alas! – one oar-blade touched the stonework of the bridge and over we went. The crew managed to cling to the overturned boat but I soon parted from it and found myself slowly sinking – I was fully clothed, in contrast to my colleagues – in an upright attitude. When the water reached halfway up my tie it stopped, and my feet landed on something. Since I was still under the arch of the bridge, I felt apprehensive lest another boat should swish through and beat me about the ears with its oars. So I thought I would wade to the bank. I took one step and disappeared from view – I had been standing on some projecting flange of the bridge pier. I scrambled back and awaited ignominious rescue by small boys (the same small boys?) hauling me over the stern of a rowing boat.

Undoubtedly the most colourful member of my crew was Ben Gunn, a huge one-eyed Hebridean. Belting down the River Wear at a ridiculously high rate of striking one would hear a panicky shout from No 2, "Och hell! The stroke's fantastic!". Most of his pronouncements began with "Och hell!" and many were wild hyperbolic statements on subjects about which he knew nothing. One example will suffice, "Och hell! There was only one good line of poetry ever written!" (He read Physics.) Pressed to reveal which line had received this supreme accolade (consigning the rest of the world of poetry to the dustbin) Ben became uncharacteristically shy. Even he could see that he had overreached himself. Eventually he was persuaded to mutter, "Och hell!

A rose-red city half as old as time . . ."

Ben was emotional. This could show itself in a warming loyalty; "Och hell! I won't row unless Pete New coxes me!" Or he could be depressed and homesick for his wife and family. On one such occasion I impishly enquired if he was "longing for his ain folk" and on another I enjoined him to "snap out of" his "Celtic Twilight". The reaction to both was similar – a great roar and a chase out into the snow. This was two parts fun to one part fear for my life because the snow was deep and Ben did not know his own strength.

Like Ben, many other undergraduates were ex-servicemen, and a number could not settle down to study after up to six years in the forces. After all, for most the armed services are five per cent danger and ninety-five per cent a training in how to waste time. One Jopling, of a family of glass manufacturers, left because, he said, Durham was interfering with his education. But there was a mix of school leavers and older students, pleasant and less pleasant, working class and middle class. J.B. Melford came from the upper middle classes and was therefore entitled to say "What?" instead of "I beg your pardon?" He had, it seemed to me, the nervous habit of affecting deafness, so that when one addressed him, the response would always be, "What? What? What do you say? What?" It was many years later when I was told that he really was a little deaf. Like Ben Gunn's lost eye, it was attributable to a war injury. Ex-servicemen rarely talked about their war experiences, and then only in a lighthearted way.

A fair number of students came from County Durham and the north of England generally – there was no other university between Leeds and Edinburgh. So there was a regional flavour, exemplified in the Geordie accent imparted to the Latin grace. With long disyllabic vowels and glottal stops,

. . . ut nos, quod satis est habentes . . .

became

. . . ut nooüs, quod sa'is est haben'es . . .

One evening the grace was read by Maxwell Gray. Maxie knew no Latin, and though full of confidence totally

174

lacked competence. Everyone from high table to waitress squirmed as he orated in a bastard Italian, waving his arms about the while. Maxie was a cockney wide boy, quite shameless in constantly entreating, "I say, old man, can you lend me a cigarette?"

My main companion at Durham was Ivor Erroll Lindsay Scott-Oldfield. He had been a naval officer for six years and like the other ex-servicemen had a wordly wisdom which equipped him to stand up to his teachers. Indeed, Scotty's classics professor (Morrison) had served under him as an Able Seaman. Bertie Colgrave, in a phonetics class, invited his audience to guess where he came from, thinking that he had disguised his origins completely. Scotty disconcerted him by accurately singing out "Birmingham!" at once. It was Scotty's intention to go on to theological college after taking his degree, and he rather fancied himself reaching the position of Archbishop of York – simply because he would then have the euphonious name Ivor Ebor. He did not quite make it that far, but he did become a clergyman and ended his career as the Director of the Royal National Institute for the Deaf.

Scotty lived on the floor below me in the keep, and we frequently had tea together, being summoned to the other's room by the cry of "I have prepared an infusion of tea!" *Inter alia* we would discuss our fellow undergraduates, and when we disapproved of someone we would agree, "What a dead loss that man is. He ought to be in Hatfield." Scotty is the only one of my contemporaries with whom I have kept in touch. We used to correspond using mad names; he was Scott-Colgrave and I was Abbott-Leech. Now we meet occasionally at events organised by the Durham University Society (President Howard Phelps).

One student looked remarkably like the Master, so much so that Scotty and I described his supposed parentage in racehorse breeding terms, 'by Macfarlane-Grieve out of Mrs. Shaw'. Another contemporary was the shy Miss Day: whatever her forename was, I called her Agnes (Agnus Dei). By contrast an outstanding figure was Miss R****** of the Jutting Breasts. Scotty and I feared that if her relevant parts were punctured with a pin they would burst with a loud bang, like a balloon. A fellow Castleman seemed to spend his entire undergraduate career canoodling with his girlfriend in the Union coffee bar. We noted that on a letter waiting for him in the porter's lodge someone had extended the initials of his forenames (E R) to EROS, and that was the name by which Scotty and I referred to him. Seeing Eros stagger off on vacation with two heavily laden suitcases, we supposed that they contained gross packets of contraceptives.

In the fullness of time we all had to stagger off on our last vacation. As Professor Abbott characteristically put it to a colleague, "Well Philipson, you can't be living in a fool's paradise all your life!" He was going round his final year students, and to me he said, "I hear you are going to be a *librarian*, New". The tone he used would have been appropriate had I been contemplating a career as a lavatory attendant.

INDEX OF PEOPLE AND PLACES

TERMS EXCLUDED: Names of parents and brother; house name "The Steppes"; "Isle of Wight"; countries and continents; names and places in songs; names of colleges; streets and buildings in towns; personal names used for shops or ships. Where possible houses are indexed under place, eg "Pyle Manor" under "Pyle".